Aim Higher!!

Don't settle for average returns!
Be active!!

Dow 85,000!!

Rare Opportunity!
A mega secular bull is in progress!
Gains of +700% by 2030!

Ultra Sector Index   Ultra Market Leaders Index
Market Leaders Index   Sector Growth Index

Marshall Schield and Trent Schield

Published by Dog Ear Publishing
4010 W. 86th Street, Ste H
Indianapolis, IN 46268
www.dogearpublishing.net

ISBN: 978-1-4575-2511-7

This book is printed on acid-free paper.

Printed in the United States of America

Foreword by; Jerry C. Wagner, President

Flexible Plan Investments, Ltd.

After following the stock market for nearly 50 years, I've seen many books predicting both fantastic returns and stomach-wrenching plunges. The production of such books is almost a cottage industry in the financial service sector.

But, this book is unique. It presents a strong case for its end goal – Dow 85,000 – just as other books have argued eloquently for their predictions. The difference is that Trent and Marshall present us with a quantitative methodology that not only seeks to improve on the prediction, but also gives us a set of defensive tools designed to defend against cyclical bear markets as well as the possibility that their prediction does not come to pass.

The thoroughness of the Schields' presentation comes as no surprise to me. I've known Marshall for 25 years, and for many of those years he was my fiercest and toughest competitor in the asset management business. Then he returned to his love of research and founded STIR. The firm went on to become a well-respected leader in the production of technical market indexes and strategies. He has lived and breathed active management for over 40 years and is the perfect person to author this book.

I started working with Marshall's sons, Troy and Trent, ten years ago. Troy has implemented the Market Leaders strategy for my firm since we co-launched it in 2008. His firm is itself a registered investment advisory firm providing asset management services. Trent joined our firm in 2008 as a regional sales manager with, responsibility for much of the western United States. He quickly moved to the number-one position on our staff of more than fifteen wholesalers.

As I said earlier, many books have been written projecting stupendous heights for stocks. The differentiator this book provides is two-fold:

1.   a method for managing each reader's portfolio that opens it to the opportunity for multiplying gains, and most importantly,
2.   defensive tools for protecting the portfolio if the prognostication proves wrong.

The method suggested to accomplish both of these goals is "Active Management." But: "What is 'active management'?"

Many confuse the phrase with the simple act of running a mutual fund populated with stock picks within the strict guidelines of a prospectus, as opposed to running an index fund, where the manager simply buys and holds the shares making up a particular stock or bond index. While there may be other definitions that have equal merit, I would look at the question in a different way – with active management being a means to adding multi-dimensionality to one's investing to better reach one's goals.

We are often told to "be a 'buy-and-hold' investor." Yet, while the phrase "buy and hold" is two words linked together by a connector; that single conjunction, "and", does not give the phrase dimensionality. Buy and hold, in its purest form, has zero dimensionality – you buy. "Holding" is not a word of action. Following this approach is passive investing in its purest form.

Graphically, zero dimensionality is a dot. It has no length, width or height – it's only a dot, just like the period at the end of this sentence. Like the period, it can appear at any place on a page – high or low. Like the return from a buy-and-hold investment, it just "is." It's the return of the underlying index and that's all there is. When the S&P is up, like it was in 2013, for example, the dot is higher. When it's down 55%, like it was in 2007-2008, that's all she wrote – you get what you see.

Most investors are one-dimensional investors. They buy and… they sell. Both verbs denote activity – buying and selling. That makes most investors active investors.

While passive investors often focus only on the state of the investment itself without dimension (i.e. the factors about the investment that caused them to buy in the first place), active investors view investing in at least a one-dimensional state. No longer just a "dot," a one dimensional line consists of at least two dots. They focus on both buy and sell factors.

Still, they differ further. Some buy and then sell after a long time, while others buy and then, within a fairly short time, they sell. One-dimensional investing, then, is like a line. And that line can be long or short.

To graduate to two-dimensional investing, as one would in drawing, where length and height are combined to form a triangle for example, one must add another component and look at direction.

A triangle has height and length. And when one views the chart of an investment, it's pretty clear what this shape signifies – a bear market.

Add a bull market and put the two together, and the two-dimensional surface becomes a full market cycle.

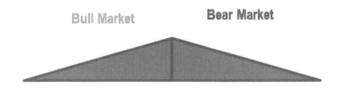

Bull Market   Bear Market

A two-dimensional investor, then, considers market direction, or the prevailing direction of prices of the individual securities, in making his or her buy and sell decisions. The market environment can actually alter the length of time that one holds the investment, whether you buy or sell at all, or even whether you reverse the process and sell short to benefit from a current or impending downturn.

Dynamic, risk-managed investing adds a whole new element – risk management – a new dimension. Dynamic, risk-managed investing is like a cube. It's three dimensional. It has width, length and height. Dynamic, risk-managed investing is many steps beyond the simple act of buying and selling. A lot more is going on.

Basic, or one-dimensional, active managers have factors that influence when to buy – just like the buy-and-hold investor – but add in a process for determining when to sell. Both the buy and the sell factors are quantitative (or solely numbers based) – no emotion, no subjectivity, just disciplined, mathematical investing.

Intermediate-level, or two-dimensional, active managers add in the directional dimension – price momentum, the potential downside, the price movement of one investment as it relates to another – all coming together to determine the position to take in an investment. Strategies can be employed that are based on following the trend, doing the opposite (mean reversion) or simply following price patterns that have historical persistency in terms of follow through.

Dynamic, risk-managed investors add in yet another dimension – the risk management dimension. Its three-dimensional practitioners incorporate advanced investment ingredients: the active reallocation of the position size in any investments to as small as zero, hedging, the use or avoidance of leverage, shifts to cash and bonds determined by volatility, tactical timing measures, and stop loss signals.

These add a whole new element of dimensionality. The result is a complete investment strategy like each of those described in this book. A strategy based on dynamic, risk-managed investing that considers not just getting invested, or just buying and selling, or even determining whether the market is moving up or down. Instead, it considers all of these elements plus the tools to actively preserve the investment in case bad luck or a bad strategy results in unintended losses.

Finally, think of each of those dynamic, risk-managed investing three-dimensional cubes, these separate dynamic, risk-managed strategies, as bricks. Combine them and you have the safety of a home. Bringing together actively managed strategies in a single portfolio, as is advocated in this volume, is designed to deliver a strategically diversified, dynamic, risk-managed portfolio, which, like your home, is intended to weather the fourth dimension – time.

Investors need the solid combination of all of the bricks to form a home, to weather the storms that roar through the financial environment over a full financial cycle – the times when the markets are up and the times when they are down. Only active management, not passive holding of investments, is multi-dimensional. And today, active management is available through a growing number of money managers and the advisory firms who employ their services.

So whether an investor's portfolio resembles a studio apartment, a modest three-bedroom home, or a far more spacious property, technological innovations can now provide the same active management advantages previously available only to high net worth clients and institutional investors.

An investor has to ask oneself, "Would I rather stand on a dot on the sidewalk out in front of my future home, or move into the multi-dimensional space inside?" The choice, as they say, is up to you.

As for me, if the Schields' target is even half right, we're in for quite a ride with our investments over the next decade. I want to be part of it, and I'm going to Aim Higher with active management!

Jerry C. Wagner, President
Flexible Plan Investments, Ltd.
Bloomfield Hills, MI

Dow 85,000! "Do not name the book that," "Everyone will think you lost it," "You have to be kidding, with all the problems in the economy, no way!!"

These were probably the nicer comments we received when we announced this book.

But consider this. Back in late 1999 or early 2000 when record highs were being made daily, money was easy to make, brokerage ads were touting "owning your own island from day trading," etc. If someone had told you that the party was over, and for the next decade stocks would lose one-fourth their value, would you have listened?

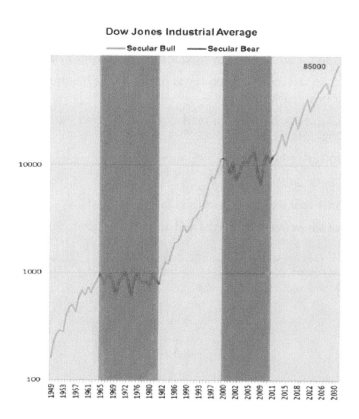

Probably not. You would have considered the advice as coming from a "nut job," someone out of touch.

Of course, that advice would have been right on, so do not be quick in prejudging. We have the experience and the data supporting a Dow 85,000 by 2030.

The market has a rhythm. It moves in long term cycles of underperformance followed by over performance. The decade of poor performance is behind us.

A new mega secular bull market has begun, one that will last decades, and producing +700% gains. It is a rare opportunity, a time to build significant wealth.

But why settle for just market returns?

Aim Higher!

Be in that top quartile that will achieve final gains three times (3X) greater than the market in this new mega bull market.

Milestone Market Calls Past Four Decades

Marshall L Schield, Chief Strategist, STIR Research LLC

1. In early 1980's named by Money Magazine as one of top four market timers for prior decade which was a tough secular bear market.

2. Buy signal generated in August 1982.

3. Avoided Crash of 1987 (stocks fell over -25% in single day), winning recognition in Barron's, USA Today and other national publications as one of the few managers to be out of the market.

4. In 1990, along with Troy Schield managed the #1 capital appreciation fund according to Lipper Analytical Services.

5. In 1997, authored the first book on sector fund investing: *"Sector Funds for Trophy Returns."*

6. Late 1998-2000, while participating in last bull market run was one of only a handful of strategist preparing for new secular bear market.

7. Avoided the majority of 2000-2002 and 2007-2009 bear market declines of over -50% and participating in 2002-2007 and 2009-2011 bull markets.

8. Sell signal on Nov. 7, 2007 (S&P 500 at 1476).

9. Buy signal on June 1, 2009 (S&P 500 at 943).

10. Bullish call on October 31, 2011, only four weeks into new secular bull market.

11. 2013 STIR Market Outlook, forecast for new all time highs and a 20% S&P move.

S&P 500 Index

Introduction

Two generations of active strategists who have survived and prospered for over 50 years. Marshall (father), Sandra, Trent and Troy Schield (sons), have spent their careers studying and observing markets, market trends and investor behavior. They are avid students of market history and investor behavior.

Besides the normal day to day analysis of market gyrations, they also had a keen perception of long term secular (often decades) moves in the market. Marshall has over 50 years of experience, spanning two secular bear markets and one secular bull. *"If I could pick between the two, secular bull markets are by far my favorite."* **Marshall Schield**

Before starting with the reason for today's book, let us rewind back to a conversation back fifteen years ago. *"We have buy signals across the board in every strategy, time to get out of cash and move back into the market,"* **Troy Schield**

That started the first discussion back in October 1998 with Troy Schield, then Vice President of Research with Schield Management Company, in charge of running the daily quantitative analysis on 50+ strategies for over 15,000 clients and $300 million under management. After a secular bull market that commenced in 1982 and gained over 900%, there had been concern that the 1998 bear market had signaled the end of the secular bull and the start of a new secular bear market. But the market had reversed itself and had begun to rally.

I recall my exact words: *"I don't believe this rally, and we are going to get whipsawed with this buy signal. This market is at extremes. But, we have to follow the analysis. Go ahead and buy back in, but be prepared to get out."* **Marshall Schield**

The good news we followed the analysis and ended up participating fully in the final blow off rally of an eighteen-year-old secular bull. Gains over the next year were in many cases triple digits! And the secular bear market did begin some eighteen months after the discussion: <u>Marshall was right, but just early,</u> but he and Troy had followed the signals to buy. Equally important they were fully prepared for the secular bear with defensive active strategies.

The research behind today's book, *"Dow 85,000! Aim Higher!"* began several years ago. In reviewing history, all of us knew that the secular bear would end and be followed by a new mega-secular bull market lasting decades: a sequence that has been repeated time and time again over the past century.

Based upon real experience, we also knew that the majority of investors would miss out on many of the extraordinary benefits of this new mega bull market. They simply would not believe it until much of the gains had already passed them by.

Our collective goal is to help investors and advisors understand that we are in a new investment era, one that will last decades, and if taken full advantage of will alter one's ultimate life style. Also, that the current opportunity for the majority of readers is truly a once in a lifetime opportunity. Sounds dramatic, but it is too true.

After great discussion, it was determined the book should convey four important messages:

1. A new mega secular bull market lasting decades with gains of +700% is in progress. One you cannot afford to miss.

2. Aim Higher: do not settle for simple market gains when much larger returns are within reach.

3. Active Indexes that strive to outperform the market with less risk are the preferred investment vehicle to take advantage of this new bull market.

4. Perspective, staying on track and winning.

Dow 85000!! Aim Higher!!

Table of Contents

FIRST MESSAGE

New Secular Bull Market

- What is the difference between a secular market and a cyclical market?

- Why should I even care?

- Bull, Bear, why not just call them rising and falling markets?

- Why is the secular bear (falling) market over after 11 years?

- New Boom, Mega Bull Market, what will cause that?

- Why 85,000? How did you get that number?

- Gain of 700%, love to hear about that!

- If we can get to a Dow 85,000 we will all be 'dancing' like the bull!

> *"The value of moments, when cast up, is immense,*
> *if well employed; if thrown away, their loss is irrevocable."*
>
> —Lord Chesterfield

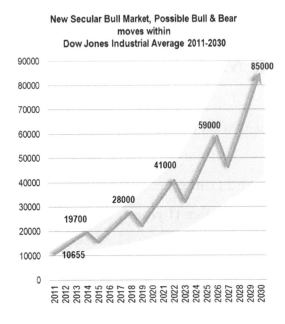

New Secular Bull Market, Possible Bull & Bear moves within Dow Jones Industrial Average 2011-2030

A new mega secular bull market is here!

Stocks will soar for the next several decades!

The Dow Jones Industrial Average could move from current levels to over 85000 by 2030!

Not in one big move, but a stair step series of cyclical bull and bear markets.

Stocks, not bonds, are the place to be.

The secular bond bull market is over, the future is in stocks.

Equity portfolios should see gains of +700%!

You can sit back, do nothing, stop reading this book and just put your dollars into an index fund and enjoy the new wealth that is headed your way.

OR
"Carpe Diem," Seize the Moment

Take full advantage of this rare opportunity (secular bulls only happen once in every 3 or 4 decades) and be smart, be active, and make your hard earned dollars work harder for you.

Why settle for just 700%, **Aim Higher**; with guidance, skill, experience, active management and hard work, +2100% is within reach.

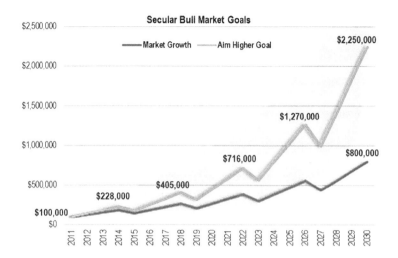

Why watch $100,000 grow to $800,000 when over $2,200,000 could be the goal!!!

In the following chapters we will explain:

- What is a secular bull market, and it's potential for you?
- Why we are in a new secular bull market!
- How we see the potential of +700% gains for the market.
- How to use active indexes to multiply the potential of this secular bull market.
- How to keep perspective, one key to success.
- How to get started: Dow85000AimHigher.com.

This is not a 'get rich quick' book or a book of gimmicks or a book about investing in exotic or unusual investments. No, we focus on the opportunities of a secular bull and active indexes that can turbo charge your returns.

"A wise man will make more opportunities than he finds."

—Sir Francis Bacon

We will strive to avoid using confusing terms or too many industry descriptions that make understanding the concepts presented difficult. However, four terms are essential and are used throughout the book and need to be described before moving forward.

- *Secular Markets*: these are long term moves in the stock market that can encompass several decades.
- *Cyclical Markets*: shorter term moves, as little as 3 to 4 months, or spanning several years.
- *Bull Markets*: a period of generally rising prices.
- *Bear Markets*: describe a period of generally falling prices or a period of no gains.

"I can't see the forest because of the trees" describes the dilemma institutional and individual investors are facing today. Investors are focused too much on specific or short term problems and trends and fail to grasp the big picture.

Investors are worrying about the next market move (trees), up or down, of 5% or 10%, and they are missing the point (forest). A **major shift is occurring: a new secular bull market with gains of +700% lasting two decades is underway!**

We will be describing a new secular bull market (a two decade period of generally rising prices) that will include a series of cyclical bull and bear markets (shorter intermediate term moves of rising and falling prices). But before you can grasp just how significant this secular bull can be to your financial future, a better understanding of the differences between secular and cyclical moves is needed.

Understanding the significance of the mega bull market will help you weather the short term market storms that will occur.

A picture is worth a thousand words, so hopefully the chart below of the last **Secular Bear Market** (lengthy period of declining prices) with a series of **cyclical bull and bear markets** (shorter time periods of rising and falling price trends) within it, illustrates the point. Obviously it wins its **title as a Secular Bear Market by losing -26% of its value over a long period of time (11+ years), and** a $100,000 investment would have declined to just $74,000. Within the secular bear, it contained **three cyclical bear markets (-49%, -56% and -19%), and two cyclical bull markets (+101%, and +102%).**

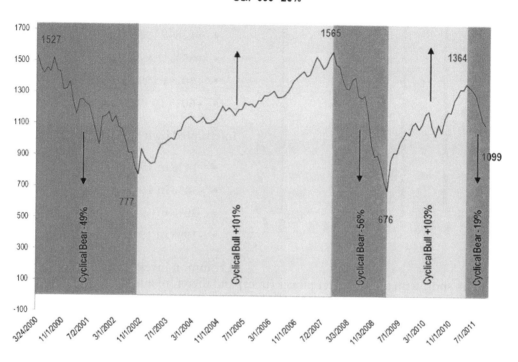

Secular bears start when optimism is at its peak (2000, the end of the last secular bull market). Investors had experienced nothing but spectacular gains up to that point. Making money was easy, too easy. The mantra was "it's time in the market, not timing the market." Extremely bad advice, any strategist worth his or her salt knew this to be false. Long periods of rising prices (secular bulls) are always followed by a lengthy period of falling prices (secular bear), a repetitive pattern that has been in existence as long as there have been investors.

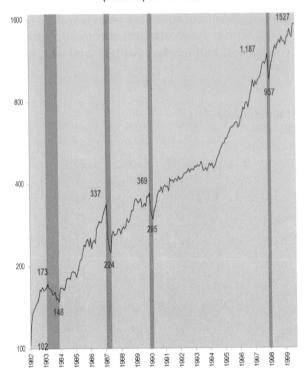

Secular Bull
(1982-2000) S&P 500 Index

Here is the exact opposite, a long term period (18+ years) of generally rising prices, **a Secular Bull market**. The 80's and 90's were extraordinarily good. The S&P 500 Index, a benchmark of performance of leading U.S. companies gained **+1400%, and** a $100,000 investment would have grown to $1,500,000.

Within this secular bull, the market experienced five **cyclical bull market moves:**

- +69% 1982-1983
- +128% 1984-1987
- +65% 1988-1990
- +302% 1991-1998
- +60% 1999-2000

Interrupted by four **cyclical bear markets:**

- -14% in 1983-1984
- -34% in 1987
- -20% in 1990
- -19% in 1998

A common investment error is to be caught up emotionally in short term stock market moves (trees) and therefore missing the major move that is occurring (the forest).

The majority of investors did not participate in the gains of the early years (1982-1987). The psychology of Secular Bull markets is they are born with despair and disbelief (feelings left over from the last secular bear market) and only after years of gains do investors gradually begin to believe in a positive future.

All secular bulls end with a state of euphoria (1999-2000), when great past returns are mistakenly extrapolated far into the future.

Success comes from clearly understanding and keeping perspective of where you are within the bigger picture.

Secular Markets: Boom or Bust

"Knowledge is Power"

—Sir Francis Bacon

Investors are very familiar with the rewards of a bull market (rising prices) and the pain of bear markets (falling prices). However, most are not familiar with the striking difference between secular bull and bear markets. One of the keys to excelling in investing is understanding that difference and then using that knowledge to take full advantage of investment opportunities.

All the popular financial magazines talk about average long term returns: how $100,000 grew to $1,110,000 over the past three decades. While that is important, it glosses over some very unpleasant facts.

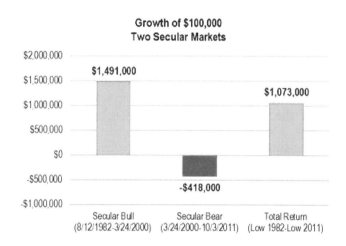

So why should investors care? Markets go up and down. True, however it is in the **secular bull markets that all the big money is made!** $100,000 grew to $1,500,000 over the first two decades!

Over the final decade, in the secular bear market a -28% decline resulted in $1,500,000 falling by $400,000.

Only savvy advisors will tell you this. Others will just point to final returns and let you live in ignorance.

"Carpe Diem," Seize the Moment

Take full advantage of this rare opportunity (secular bulls only happen once in every 3 or 4 decades) and be smart, be active, and make your hard earned dollars work harder for you.

New Secular Bull a Rare Opportunity

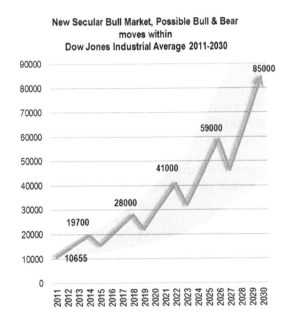

New Secular Bull Market, Possible Bull & Bear moves within Dow Jones Industrial Average 2011-2030

The typical investor has a total investment horizon of only 30 or 40 years to **build** wealth. Often starting in their late 20's through their late 60's, this is the time of accumulating and building wealth. The closer retirement comes the more conservative the investment strategy becomes and preservation of principal becomes more important than growth of capital.

Here's the hard facts and their implication:

- As investors we have only 3 or 4 decades in which to build great wealth;
- And secular bull and bear markets will each last 1 or possibly 2 decades.

Therefore, if you are lucky (depending upon when your investment horizon started), you may experience the strong tail wind of a secular bull market twice during the wealth building years. For others, now in their 40's, 50's and 60's, as a practical matter, the new secular bull market may be their last!

Today, many indicators point to the early stages of a new **Secular Bull**. Like past secular bull markets, it could encompass 19 to 20 years and gain over 700%!

We have an opportunity where a $100,000 portfolio can grow to $800,000 by the time it is finished, and that is just with market returns. We will be introducing actively managed indexes that will Aim Higher!

DOW 85000! AIM HIGHER!

New Secular Bull has Started: Old Secular Bear is Dead

So what points to the end of the secular bear market (2000-2011) and the start of a new secular bull market?

- History shows how past secular bear markets have ended.
- Pessimism is at record highs (a necessity for the birth of a new secular bull market).
- Valuations are at historical lows.
- Starting in obscurity, with no bells or whistles to mark the birth.

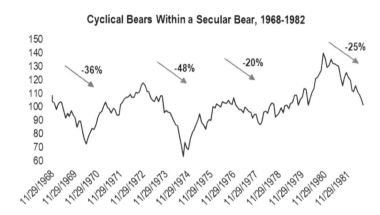

Cyclical Bears Within a Secular Bear, 1968-1982

Secular Bears end with a whimper. The final cyclical bear market (1980-1982), one of four, did not drop the most (just over 25%). In comparison the 1970 and 1973 cyclical bears fell 36.1% and 48.2%.

The absolute low price point for any secular bear does not occur at the actual end. The price low is made years before. In the 1968-1982 secular bear, the price low was on 10/3/74, eight years before the final cyclical bear market low in 1982.

Many investors think the end of a secular bear would be its absolute low point in price. However, the end comes when pessimism and despair are at peaks and valuations are at lows.

Valuation Low

Measuring emotional levels is difficult. However, one indicator of investor optimism or pessimism about the future is what price they are willing to pay for future earnings: the Price/ Earnings ratio. If investors are optimistic and feeling euphoric about the coming years and decade they will pay more for these optimistic feelings, yielding high P/E ratios. It is quite the opposite when investors are wallowing in gloom, doom, fear and pessimism. The future looks unreliable, shaky and therefore, P/E ratios are low.

Remember, secular bears start when optimism is at its peak and ends with total despair, therefore the pattern or trend of P/E ratios should reflect investor emotions moving from optimism to pessimism: pessimism is at its greatest when the P/E ratio is at its lowest. All the Secular Bull Markets ended when P/E ratios were at their lowest. The chart shows the downward slide in P/E ratios during the last three secular bear markets, falling from high levels of optimism (end of last secular bull) to their lows at the end of the secular bear, a low in valuation.

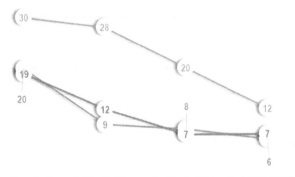

FALLING P/E RATIOS IN SECULAR BEAR MARKETS

— — 1929-49   — — 1968-82   — —2000-11

Start of Secular Bear   1st Cyclical Bear   2nd Cyclical Bear   End of Secular Bear

A reader studying the graph could say 'But wait, P/E ratios in 2011 were substantially higher than they were at the end of the previous secular bears. Why shouldn't we wait until they hit 6 or 7 to signal the end?'

Good point, but consider this:

1. Look at the relative decline in P/E ratios: from 1929 to 1949 the ratio fell 70%, during the 1968-1982 the ratio endured a 68% drop, and most recently, 2000-2011 P/E's fell 60%.

2. If it makes you feel more comfortable, just months prior to the 2000 peak, the P/E ratio hit a high of 34. From that point until the 2011 low, P/E's fell 65%, in line with previous percentage declines.

Another Sign of Pessimism, Record Corporate Earnings are being Ignored

Another common theme during secular bears is ignoring the good news. Investors focus on the negative: unemployment is high, companies are not hiring, people are losing their houses, I can not get a loan, etc., and the news quite often reinforces this pessimism with negative stories of plants closing, losing jobs overseas, etc.

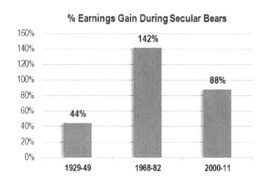

A study several years ago polled investors, asking if they knew how well the market had been doing. Over 50% felt 2009 and 2010 were down years. Factually, stocks advanced 23% in 2009 and 13% in 2010.

With all the headlines of gloom and doom and falling prices, investor perception is that corporate earnings would also be in significant decline. That is not true. Corporate earnings are on the rise, and investors in their despair ignore this.

Not only are they on the rise, but company earnings typically are at record highs!

- During the Depression and the following bear markets, earnings in the 1930's and 1940's actually grew.
- The 1968-1982 secular bear, with rampant inflation, Vietnam, Watergate, etc, saw corporate earnings more than double.
- 2000-2011, two recessions, 9/11, and the Great Recession, saw corporate earnings again almost double, rising 88%.

During cyclical bear markets within a longer term secular bear market, it is very common for corporate earnings to suffer large losses, especially during economic recessions. It happened in each of three previous secular bears, however, investors continue to live in fear and then ignore the improvement in earnings when it does occur. In 2011, corporate earnings were at all-time highs, but stock prices remained 30% below their old highs.

Investor Behavior reaches Bearish Extremes

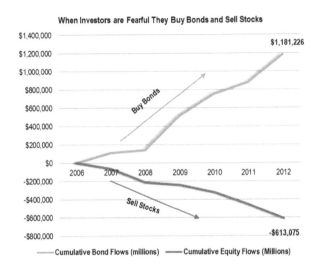

When Investors are Fearful They Buy Bonds and Sell Stocks

Source: Investment Company Institute

Secular bear markets end when fear is at an extreme. Another way to measure the level of investor pessimism is to look at investor behavior. Several old adages pop up: "Actions speak louder than words," or "Pay no attention to what people say, but pay close attention to what they do."

So what actions have investors been doing, especially at the end of the secular bear and the start of this secular bull? Are their actions bullish or still bearish, still fearful, or still scared?

Investors seek out the safety of bonds and sell stocks when they are fearful. When investors are optimistic they buy equities with greater potential for growth and sell bonds which have lower potential for gains.

Investor behavior has reached bearish extremes. Over the six-year period shown investors made new purchases of +$1 trillion in bond funds (seeking safety) and liquidated over a half a trillion dollars in domestic equity funds.

Extremely bearish, high levels of pessimism exist. Investors were dumping equities and buying record amounts of low yielding bonds.

It appears investors bearish behavior finally peaked in 2012. During 2013 (not shown in graph) with bond prices falling (yields rising) and stocks advancing, investors had net liquidations of $81 billion in bond funds and added almost twice that, $161 billion, to equity funds.

Investor Behavior reaches Bearish Extremes

Actually, the level of fear or pessimism has been higher than that reflected in the massive inflow into bonds and the exodus from stocks shown previously. Money could be flowing into bonds because yields are so attractive. Money could be fleeing stocks because of falling prices. Both could have explained the dramatic inflow and outflows. But that was not the case.

	Cumulative Bond In Flows (millions)	Yields 10 Year Treasury
Dec-06		4.71%
2007	$108.327	4.04%
2008	$137.408	2.25%
2009	$516.963	3.85%
2010	$752.520	3.30%
2011	$877.623	1.89%
2012	$1.181.226	1.78%

Normally fear of losing money in equities or high yields drive investors to bonds. Yet the move to bonds was clearly not for their high yield. The very safe 10-Year Treasury Bond yield fell 63% from 4.7% to 1.8%. The yields in 2011 and 2012 were insufficient to even keep pace with inflation. Bond investors were losing purchasing power.

The flight to bonds was a flight to safety. Investors were fearful.

	Annual Equity Out Flows (Millions)	Gain/ Losses S&P 500 Index
Dec-06		
2007	($65.283)	4%
2008	($148.806)	-38%
2009	($29.369)	23%
2010	($81.182)	13%
2011	($132.467)	0%
2012	($155.968)	13%

Money can flow out of equities because of fear (typically falling prices), which it did in late 2007 and 2008 when the market suffered a huge fall of over 50%. Not surprisingly investors sold riskier stocks and sought shelter in bonds (safer).

But since the March lows of 2009, stocks have risen 100% through 2010, but investors still sold in fear. 2011 ended as a flat year, but suffered a bear market midyear. It is understandable why nervous investors liquidated. But 2012 was a great year for stocks with double digit gains, yet investors actually stepped up the pace of selling stocks. Fear is the reason.

When investors, by their actions, choose to accept a low yielding bond, almost guaranteeing a loss in purchasing power, over equities, which are hitting record profits and are at the lowest P/E's in over two decades, one can only conclude that the market has seen bearish extremes in investor behavior!

Secular Bull Markets Begin in Obscurity!

This new secular bull market certainly fills that bill.

From the lows of March 2009, through the highs of 2011, the market staged a spectacular cyclical bull market move of over +100%. It was great for those still participating, and equity account balances doubled in value. As we mentioned previously, this gain was largely ignored or failed to change the perception of the investing public.

But what occurred after the 2011 peak and how it has been treated by the talking heads in the financial media is meaningful. A bear market occurred. A global bear market occurred. But you would not know it by listening to the press. The domestic bear market was completely ignored. Even years later, writers and analysts continue to believe that the bull market begun in 2009 was still ongoing.

By that omission, the popular press is missing all the signs that the 2000 secular bear market ended in 2011 with one final whimper. The whimper was a small bear market, one that has gone unnoticed by many, but a typical sign of the end of a secular bear market.

In each of the prior secular bears, 1929-1949, and 1968-1982, the final cyclical bear market was shallow compared to the others.

2011 Bear Market Declines

Conclusion: Why the Secular Bear (2000-2011) is Finally Over

Summary: Unfortunately a bell does not ring signaling either the end of a secular bear market or the start of a new mega bull market. The end can only be identified in hindsight. As students of history and survivor's of a previous secular bear market, we look for "markers," signs of <u>excessive pessimism signaling the end.</u>

Markers

- **Time**: almost 12 years of no gains is similar in length to the 13 years of the previous secular bear.

- **Price/Earnings Ratios fall over 65%:** similar in falls to the 1929-1949 and 1968-1982 secular bears.

- **Profit Growth Ignored:** Corporate profits continue to grow during secular bears.

- **Record Earnings Ignored:** 2011 corporate profits were up 88% since the start of the secular bear.

- **High levels of Fear:** A stampede out of equities and high inflows into the safety of bonds: over $1 trillion into bond funds, and $.5 trillion out of equity funds.

- **Last Cyclical Bear in Secular Bear is often the Smallest**: this follows the pattern of both of the prior secular bears. The 2000-2011 secular bear had three cyclical bears, -49.2%, - 56.8%, and -19.4%, with the smallest being the last.

Excessive pessimism by investors marks the end of the secular bear and the birth of a secular bull. All secular bull markets begin when investors memories of the last mega bull market have faded entirely and they continue to extrapolate the pain and frustration of the bear markets into the future. That is where we were in late 2011 and are today—pessimism trumps optimism.

Secular bull markets begin in obscurity and high levels of pessimism, rise in confidence with repetition, eventually reaching a state of euphoria!

The New Boom, the New Secular Bull Market!!

What's ahead? What will spark the next big boom? With pessimism high, investors have little hope of another great long-term stock rally. We believe all this pessimism is wrong. Conventional wisdom that we are in an extended period of subpar growth is wrong. That many experts believe investors should be prepared for a 'new normal' of below average returns for the next decade is simply wrong.

A funny thing about bull markets, they never announce themselves. A bell does not go off somewhere signaling a change in direction from secular bear to secular bull. It does not appear on our calendars. We suddenly do not come to a new day and see a reminder that today is the start of a new mega bull trend.

Big powerful bull markets (18-20 years or longer) are a breed by themselves; they are not just rebounds in a secular bear. **These new bulls are the result of the world changing in surprising ways that fundamentally alter the future**. They come as a pleasant surprise to investors, gradually changing their pessimism to optimism, and driving prices to new highs that are hard to imagine at the onset.

Mega bulls follow mega bears, like the mega bear that started in 2000 and lasted twelve years. Mega bulls last longer and wealth grows. So forget all the pessimism and be open to thinking about several fundamental changes that are occurring right now that could drive this new secular bull market! We explore several trends that will propel this market higher, and as the bull market unfolds, we are sure new trends and breakthrough inventions will add even more fuel to the move higher.

The New Boom What might Trigger it?

On Wall Street there is an old saying that states "while the market doesn't always repeat itself exactly, it often rhymes." Applying that knowledge, it is easy to see that each of the new mega boom markets of the last century have had some strong similarities.

First the obvious. Each mega boom followed a terrible, long, grueling secular bear market that included several recessions, subpar economic growth, often war, and terrible stock market returns.

Second, every new mega boom has a trigger. A new innovation or breakthrough is needed.

- Mega boom of +700% in 1915-1929 we can thank Henry Ford's concept of mass production that led to new jobs and more affordable products.
- Mega boom of 1949-1968, again a +700% rally was launched with the end of World War II, start of a baby boom and a move to the suburbs and tract housing (an innovation).
- 1982-2000 mega boom of +1400% came from technology, first with the development of the

microprocessor, which led to the personal computer, lap tops, cell phones, and the internet!

Obviously, a lot more breakthroughs occurred than just the few mentioned. However, it is indisputable, that new innovation or some sort of breakthrough have ramifications that are so large that they take us places we could not conceive of at the moment. In 1982, with the birth of a new super boom, who would have imagined that a "microprocessor" would be the great grandfather to cell phones? A phone that did not have a cord and that you could use in your car or around the world.

Conceived of by 'Dick Tracy' in the comics as he talked into his wristwatch in 1982, by 2000 it was a necessity for hundreds of millions.

Technology Breakthrough (Fracking) and Cheap Domestic Energy

Just a few years ago, experts were talking about peak oil (the eventual day that the world's oil production peaks) which would collide with rapid growth in energy demand from emerging markets like China and India. This gloom and doom scenario included forecasts of long gas lines and a rapid rise in prices that would doom all hopes of global growth.

Fast forward to today, and the U.S. is in an energy boom. Over the past several years, our production of petroleum and natural gas has risen by 33%, and imports have fallen by over 40%, to a 25 year low. <u>Biggest surprise in November 2012 the U.S. passed Saudi Arabia as the world's largest oil producer!</u>

The U.S. has perfected 'fracking'; this technology has opened massive reserves of shale gas and oil sands to development, not only leading to what was once unimaginable, energy independence, but the real possibility of 30 to 50 years of cheap and dependable energy. And that may be a low estimate. Fracking turned the U.S. into the world's second largest natural gas producer, #1 in proven reserves, and has increased supply enough to meet current U.S. consumption for the next 100 years.

The U.S. is primed to become the world's dominate energy powerhouse for decades to come. "It is not just the huge reserves we have underground. No one else has our predictable cocktail of infrastructure already in place, know-how, relative abundance of water, and a favorable royalty regime that gives landowners a stake in the exploration game." **Tim Parker, manager T .Rowe Price natural-resource portfolios.**

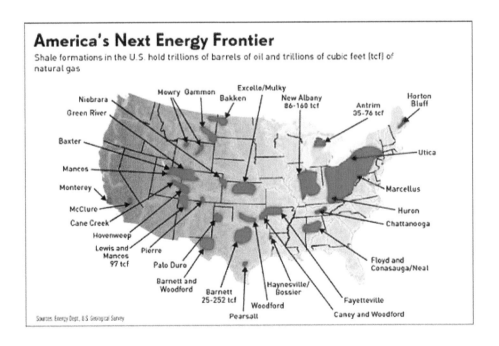

America's Next Energy Frontier
Shale formations in the U.S. hold trillions of barrels of oil and trillions of cubic feet (tcf) of natural gas

Cheap Domestic Energy Means More Jobs, "Millions"

The number of major shale fields in the U.S is well over a dozen, from the Marcellus field covering parts of New York and Pennsylvania in the east, to the Bakken field in North Dakota and Montana in the north to three different fields in Texas, Oklahoma, and New Mexico in the south, to the Monterey field in California. Exploration, development and distribution of the oil and gas will mean millions of jobs.

Hard to believe? Take a look at comments from the Governor of California, a home to green energy conservation enthusiasts, but also home to the Monterey Shale Formation in central California :

"On the subject of hydraulic fracturing (fracking), Brown said that process would be regulated through a process that "listens to people but also wants to take advantage of the great opportunities we have.

"The oil industry could not have put it better — and probably would not have put it differently.

Brown is an environmentalist, but his eyes are open. He knows that California is sitting on a vast Mother Lode of shale oil that, if tapped, could produce an economic boom in parts of the state that need it most. The Monterey Shale Formation, estimated to hold some fifteen billion barrels of recoverable oil, runs several hundred miles through the middle of the state, roughly following on the western side of the San Joaquin Valley.

In the same week Brown made his comments, a group of University of Southern California researchers and the Communications Institute, a Los Angeles based think tank, issued a study gauging the formation's economic potential. The numbers are impressive. It found that exploiting Monterey shale could generate up to 2.8 million new jobs and add 14% to the state's GDP in 2020, near the peak of production.

Those jobs would include many outside the oil patch, such as those in industries that produce drilling technology and transport oil. But plenty of employment would be near the drilling — in counties that have some of the highest chronic joblessness in the state." Investor's Business Daily, March 18, 2013

This is just one shale field among many. If one field can add 2.8 million good paying jobs, multiple that many times over for all the fields in the U.S.

From Rustbelt to a Smokestack Revolution

Manufacturing is beginning to explode in the U.S. A tidal shift from a nation exporting jobs and importing products to a nation producing more and exporting more is occurring. Several key factors are causing this smokestack revolution.

First, the U.S. energy boom, especially in natural gas, has pushed natural gas price down from over $11 per thousand cubic feet to below $3. This has caught the attention of the big manufacturer's that are reliant on natural gas to produce their products: chemical and steel producers are two examples. DuPont and Dow Chemical have already announced plans to invest $4 billion in a new plant in Texas that would hire 2,000 new workers.

Our domestic steel industry gets a double injection of good news. Not only does this energy intensive business gain from abundant and cheap natural gas used in making pipes and other products, but these same products are integral to energy drilling, and transportation (pipelines).

Toilets! We have never really given a lot of thought to the manufacturing process of a toilet, but low energy prices play a part. A toilet is really a large piece of ceramic. It takes a tremendous amount of heat to make ceramics. Currently the majority of toilets are made abroad, but with cheap gas prices here, those plants and jobs are headed (no pun intended) back here.

The trickledown effect of all the different ways cheap and abundant natural gas will encourage manufacturing management decisions to build and produce here is probably impossible to imagine or totally quantify at this time. But with huge energy reserves available at cheap prices for the next 30 to 50 years, where would you want to build your manufacturing plant? It's a no brainer, here in the U.S.

From Rustbelt to a Smokestack Revolution (continued)

Another reason for the smokestack revolution is that the U.S. is becoming more competitive. China, after years of wages rising 15% or more per year, versus stagnant wage growth here, is losing its competiveness. Also hurting countries like China are soaring industrial land costs. The average cost per square foot in China is over $10 per square foot, and in big coastal cities, like Shenzhen, it rises to $21. In comparison, industrial land costs $1.30 per square foot in Tennessee and $4.65 in North Carolina.

Experts estimate that the difference in manufacturing costs between the U.S. and Chinese coastal cities will fall to less than 10% to 15%. But there are more reasons than just these cost comparisons to move manufacturing back home.

Remember the disruptions in the supply chains due to the massive earth quakes and tsunami in Japan and the massive floods in Indonesia? Apple suffered production disruptions do to the lack of screens from Japan. Domestic auto makers slowed down auto work here because of the lack of certain parts from Japan. The floods in Indonesia slowed chip manufacturing resulting in a shortage of certain types of computers for sale in the U.S.

Other competitive reasons contribute to the smokestack revolution. With supply chains in the U.S., manufactures are closer to the world's biggest consumer market. Companies with domestic production can more quickly react to changes in consumer behavior and changes produced from innovation. Also growing in importance is the danger from theft of intellectual property. If product and processes are manufactured domestically the opportunity for intellectual theft is lessened.

U.S. retailers want a shorter supply chain, and with the cost of production increasing in Asia and high unemployment here, businesses move back home, employment picks up, adding more retail customers, a self propelling cycle.

While the trend in off shoring has gone on for the past several decades, the tide is shifting to re-shoring!

Demographics Actually a Tailwind

A common bearish perception is that the aging baby boomers are going to be a tough headwind for the market to buck over the coming decades. The reasoning goes like this: baby boomers will be liquidating higher risk stocks and moving to the safety of bonds as they reach retirement age. This ongoing liquidation of stocks will put a lid on equity prices.

Not so fast. Let us take a closer look at this assumption and what could be wrong with it. The baby boomers are defined as those born in the years 1946-1964, thus giving us an age group from 49 to 67 (as of 2013).

- Just because a boomer hits retirement age, that will not cause a 100% liquidation from equities. The shift from equities to bonds will be gradual and occur over decades. The table illustrates a thirty year spread from an aggressive stock /bond allocation of a 30 year old to a conservative allocation of a 65 year old at retirement. The closer the date to retirement the percentage invested in bonds rises and the percentage in equities declines.
- A 65 year old investor would have a 50% allocation to stocks, while a younger 35 year old investor would be more aggressive and have a larger allocation of 76% to stocks. Over a 30 year period, an investor would see a decline in equity investments from a high of 76% to 50%. That is less than a 1% decrease in equity exposure per year. This is very different from the forecasts of massive 100% stock liquidation.
- Boomers just suffered through the 'The Lost Decade' of no equity returns or losses. Account balances are less than planned, and investors are looking for ways to catch up. Bond yields are at record lows, therefore the urge to shift allocations to bonds from stocks is not really on the horizon at the moment nor will it be for most of the coming secular bull market.
- Also factor in the possible change in boomer behavior once they realize the stock market is in a mega boom (rising prices) and bonds in a secular bear (falling prices). Boomers will be in no hurry to shift out of their high returns in equities into low interest paying bonds.

Typical Allocations by Age				
Age	35	45	55	65
Stocks	76%	73%	62%	50%
Bonds	24%	27%	38%	50%

Here come the Millennials to Drive Stocks and the Economy Higher

Another positive in the changing demographics are the "Millennial". This is the group born approximately between1975-1995. It is a bigger group than the boomers, 86 million strong. This group is just beginning to fund their retirement accounts. As they grow older, so will their pay, total dollar contributions and possibly even their savings rate. With the popularity of target date funds being default investment options at many companies, this will automatically put a substantial portion of their contributions into equities. The ideal target date fund for this group will be in the range from 2040 to 2060, where 70% or more is invested in stock funds.

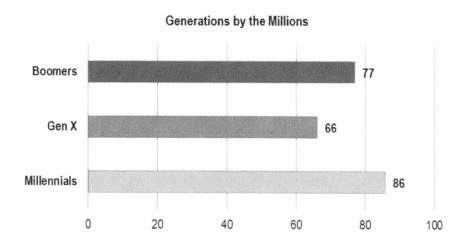

So, while the boomers stock allocations may be falling by 1% per year, the millennials will be adding 70% of their new contributions to stocks!

The Millennial generation has already made a big mark on one industry: education. Student enrollment on U.S. campuses grew by 30% from 2000-2011. This promoted a building boom on college campuses nationwide. But that may be just the first wave of their impact on the economy. After school comes jobs, family formations, new cars, new homes, etc.

More Positive Demographics: MY ratio Bullish for Stocks & the Economy

"Housing could be the next major industry to benefit from their (Millennial) size and maturation, but Wall Street could reap the biggest rewards. The <u>MY ratio, which compares the size of the middle-aged population (M) of 35-to-49 year olds with that of the young-adult population (Y), ages 20 to 34 explains why</u>.

Middle-aged folks have higher incomes than younger people, and a greater urgency to save for retirement. They invest their savings, which drives up stock prices. When the MY ratio is rising, meaning the older cohorts outnumber the younger, the stock market typically does well. The ratio has been falling since 2000, which has exerted a drag on stock prices.

Alejandra Grindal, a senior international economist at Ned Davis Research, notes *"the MY ratio will bottom in 2015 and then rise through 2029."* Barron's, April 29, 2013 cover story 'On the Rise' p. 24

<u>There exists a strong correlation between trends in the MY ratio and secular market moves</u>: the last two secular bear markets (1968-1982 with a -6% loss and 2000-2011 falling -28%) began when the MY ratio turned down, and ended when the ratio began moving higher. The last secular bull market (1982-2000 gaining 1400%) occurred when the MY ratio was rising sharply and ended when the ratio's trend turned down. The MY ratio will be rising for the majority of the new secular bull, and will top out in 2029-2031, near the possible top we see in 2030!

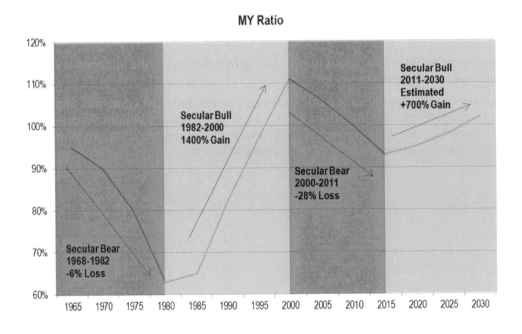

MY Ratio

Dow 85000! Aim Higher!

Secular Bear Market in Bonds will be good for Stocks

Today, interest rates are being kept artificially low by the Federal Reserve in an effort to stimulate the economy. When the Fed eventually succeeds, the artificially low rates will cease to exist and rates will rise to more normal levels. How high will rates go? The following table illustrates where rates are today versus an average of rates during the last economic recovery, 12/2002-6/2007.

	Current Rates (Summer 2014)	Peak Rates During Last Economic Recovery (12/2001-6/2007)	Percentage Point Difference in Rates
10-Year Treasury	2.40%	5.25%	2.8
20-Year Treasury	3.00%	5.60%	2.6

As bond yields climb, existing bond prices have to decline to remain competitive. Eventually, the economy will recover, and expand, interest rates will rise, but just how far will bond prices fall?

	5 Years to Maturity Bond Losses	10 Years to Maturity Bond Losses	15 Years to Maturity Bond Losses
A 2 percentage point rise in rates	-10%	-16%	-20%
A 3 percentage point rise in rates	-15%	-25%	-33%

The fall in bond prices will not occur over night, but over many years, creating a secular bear market for bonds. Investors facing losses in bonds while experiencing gains in stocks will begin to rotate out of bonds into equities.

This has been labeled the Great Rotation. The 'Great' is the expectation that a good part of the $1.2 trillion which moved into bonds (12/06-12/12) will become new buying dollars for stocks, pushing prices higher.

Deficit Trends and Secular Markets

Surpluses tend to be a positive while deficits a negative is certainly true on an individual basis, and appears to be true for nations also. Nations run two types of surpluses or deficits: fiscal and trade.

- Running larger fiscal deficits to stimulate the economy during recessions is a common theme and one practiced globally since 2008. But during robust times, the trend will be for smaller deficits or even a surplus.

- Trade Exports are reflective of U.S. competitiveness abroad (representing foreign demand for U.S. goods and services), creating jobs in the U.S., increased corporate profits, and GDP (Gross Domestic Product) growth. Imports reflect demand for foreign goods and services, but rising imports subtract from GDP growth. A trade deficit occurs when we import more than we export.

A falling trend line (because they are in negative territory) means the deficits are rising as a percentage of GDP (bad news) while a rising trend line indicates the twin deficits are becoming smaller as a percentage of GDP, which is good news!

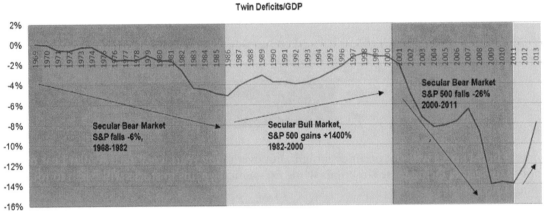

Another case of causation or correlation: long secular stock market trends mirror the direction in the twin deficits relative to GDP.

- From 1968-1982 the market went through a secular bear market of 14 years, -6% losses, and the trend in the twin deficits was also falling, trending lower.

- An 18 year secular bull with gains of 1400% then occurred, mirrored by a rising trend (deficits were becoming a smaller part of GDP) in twin deficits/GDP. The twin deficit/GDP was improving from a -5% of GDP to -1% of GDP. Stocks rallied sharply.

- This was followed by a sharp negative increase in the twin deficits, trade deficit worsened and fiscal deficits went through the roof. The twin's deficit went from just -1% of GDP to -14% of GDP by 2011. Over the same time, stocks went through a mega bear market falling 28%.

- **Since 2011, the trend has been for smaller deficits in fiscal and trade balances (therefore a rising trend line), good news for the economy, profits and the stock market!** It is the start of a new secular bull market for stocks.

Cheap Energy, Re-Shoring and smaller Twin Deficits

Ships sailing north from Chile are bringing an unusual cargo to the U.S.: chemical factories. The world's largest producer of methanol is disassembling two of its Chilean factories and rebuilding them in Louisiana. Scores of other companies plan to spend $100 billion to build or expand chemical plants in the U.S. Five years ago the trend was just the opposite.

The resurgence of the U.S. chemical industry can be explained in just four words: abundant **cheap natural gas**. The fracking boom has made the U.S. the lowest-cost chemical producer outside of the Middle East.

Employment in chemicals is sharply rising after falling 29% over the past three decades. The American Chemistry Council expects the industry will need 46,000 more workers by decade's end. Investments by chemical companies will generate an additional 1.7 million jobs in construction and other industries.

The U.S. logged a **trade surplus** of $800 million in chemicals in 2012, the first time since 2001. Expectations are that this trade surplus could balloon to $46 billion by 2020!

This is just one example of how interrelated several of the points are that are leading the U.S. to a New Boom.

Exploration, drilling and moving cheap energy will produce millions of jobs. Millions of more jobs will be created in industries that will benefit from abundant cheap energy. More people working leads to more taxes being paid to the Federal Government and less paid in unemployment benefits: a smaller fiscal deficit.

In this lone example, the U.S. moves from a trade deficit in chemicals to a trade surplus: $46 billion by 2020. This is just one industry. How many other industries will experience similar favorable trends?

A new boom is here, giving us the base for a new secular bull market.

Conclusion: New Boom and Secular Bull Market!

New mega bulls are the result of the world changing in surprising ways that fundamentally alter the future.

- Technology breakthrough, Fracking
    - ✓ U.S. leader in oil production
    - ✓ World's largest reserves of natural gas
    - ✓ U.S. primed to be world's dominant energy powerhouse for decades to come
- Cheap Natural Gas
    - ✓ 30 to 50 years of cheap dependable energy
    - ✓ Development will lead to millions of new high paying jobs
    - ✓ Bakken field in North Dakota has driven unemployment rate to 3.2%, the lowest in the country in 2012.
- Cheap Energy leads to a 'Smokestack Revolution'
- 'Re Shoring' will replace 'Off Shoring'
- Demographics a Tailwind
    - ✓ Boomers will not be a major negative for the stock market.
    - ✓ Millennial will drive economy and stocks higher.
    - ✓ MY ratio on the rise from 2015-2029, an economic stimulus.
    - ✓ Trend direction in MY ratio corresponds with secular markets (bull and bear) for past 70 years, a rising MY trend equals rising stock prices.
- Secular Bear market in Bonds will be good for stocks (stocks are the better alternative!)
- Great Rotation (money will flow out of bond funds into equity funds)
- Twin Deficits trend is improving, deficits will be a smaller % of GDP in future years, therefore a rising trend line. Secular stock market moves mirror the trend direction in Twin Deficits to GDP for the past 100 years.

A Cycle of Stock Market Underperformance Followed by Over Performance	
1929-49 Under	-57%
1949-68 Over	700%
1968-82 Under	-5%
1982-2000 Over	1400%
2000-2011 Under	-26%
2011-2030 Over estimate	700%

For the past century the market has consistently followed a repeating pattern of long cycles of underperformance where the rate of return is far lower than the historical average followed by an over performance cycle that produces higher-than-average returns. We are in the early days of a new over performance cycle that should take us +700% higher over the coming two decades!

Why 85,000? How we got the Number!

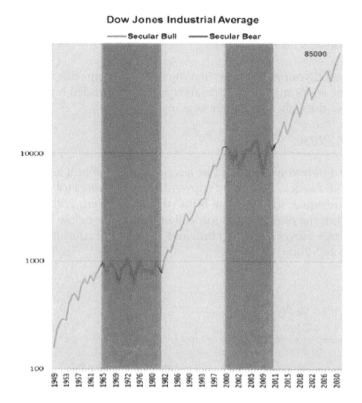

Dow Jones Industrial Average
— Secular Bull   — Secular Bear

Goals of 85,000 on the Dow or 8800 for the S&P 500 Index seem unimaginable to many people.

Here are some of the comments we received when announcing this book:

"It's just not possible. It's a pipe dream!"

"Gains of over 700%, how can you possibly support that fantasy?"

"A rising market for the next couple of decades? Not possible."

"It's different this time; it's not like the good old days of the '90's."

"The country has too many large problems today that make such a big move impossible!"

Now for the good news!

All of these statements represent convential investment "wisdom."

Yet, we will show that both the fundamentals and history support the goal.

Please keep in mind that the current investor mentality is still focused around surviving a mega bear, a 12 year secular bear market in which the market fell by over 50% on two occasions. It is very hard for investors to wrap their mind around potentially large gains when the experience of losing half the value of their investments is still fresh in their minds.

Let's review the last two secular bull markets for reference points of what could occur this time.

Why 85,000 Target?

Time was a critical element in determining the target of 85000 in the Dow. You need a benchmark that projects how long the mega secular bull will last, before the next secular bear market. With only two secular bulls in the past 6+ decades, there is a limited number of examples to go on: the 1949-1968 Bull lasted 19+ years, and the 1982-2000 Bull lasted 18 years.

Another yardstick was the MY Ratio (middle aged/young adults). When the trend is rising with more middle aged consumers than young adults, the economy and stock market have also trended higher. The MY Ratio trend is expected to move higher through 2029 before peaking.

<u>**We chose to use 19 years as an estimate: 2011-2030.**</u>

Secular bulls do not travel in a straight upward trajectory; there will be a series of cyclical bull and bear markets. A chart of secular Bulls looks like a series of stair steps upward, large advances followed by modest declines. And not all of the steps are equal: some cyclical bulls will be short term, others long, some will sport triple digit gains (rare) but the majority in double digits. The table below illustrates the shortest, longest, and the small to large moves of cyclical bull and bear markets during the past two secular Bull markets (1949-68 and 1982-2000).

Cyclical Bull Markets in Secular Bulls

Time Period	% Gain (S&P 500 Index)	# of months	
10/7/66-11/28/68	48%	26	Smallest Gain
10/11/90-7/17/98	302%	93	Largest Gain & Longest Rally
8/12/82-10/10/83	69%	14	Shortest rally

Cyclical Bear Markets in Secular Bulls

Time Period	% Loss	# of months	
10/10/83- 7/24/84	-14%	10	Smallest Decline
8/25/87-12/4/87	-34%	3	Largest Decline
7/17/98-8/31/98	-19%	1½	Shortest Decline
8/2/56-10/22/57	-22%	15	Longest Decline

In both previous secular bulls, there were typically 5 steps up (cyclical bulls) and 4 steps down (cyclical bears). In building a chart to illustrate the Dow reaching 85000, we simply used **the median size moves, both in time and price**.

	Median Gain or Loss	Median Time of Advance or Decline
Cyclical Bull Advances	85%	36 months
Cyclical Bear Declines	-22%	7 months

Why 85,000? Rising Earnings

Earnings: Once you make an intelligent forecast on length of time for the mega bull market, you can move on to the next key element, what earnings will be like in 2030. During the last secular bear market (2000-11), which included two recessions, with the last being so large, lengthy and deep it earned the name "The Great Recession," earnings rose. For the S&P 500 Index, a benchmark of large American companies, earnings gained 88% or 5.2% per year over the 12 year period.

Secular bulls, on the other hand, may contain a recession or two, but historically they have been short and shallow. The majority of the time they are periods of growth and prosperity and earnings rise even faster. During the last secular bull (1982-2000) earnings rose over 300%. Impressive, however it was only an annualized rate of 8.1%, just 50% greater than during the 2000-11 period.

Our forecast is conservative. We estimate the rate of earnings growth to pick up from the secular bear rate of 5.2% and grow at a rate of 7.2%, which is less than the last secular bull market.

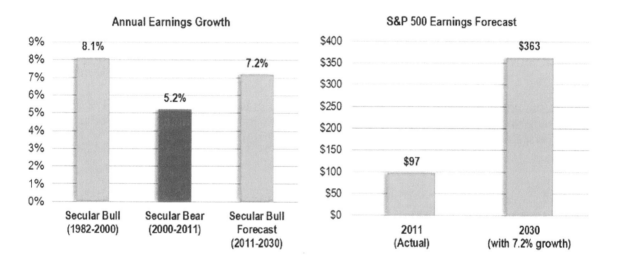

If you start with the 2011 S&P earnings of $97 and grow them at an annual rate of 7.2%, a slower growth rate than that of the last secular bull market, over the next 19 years S&P 500 earnings grow to $363.00.

Why 85,000? Rising Price/Earnings Ratio

A partner with earnings in determining price levels is the P/E ratio. During mega bear markets, as investors become depressed P/E ratios fall. During mega bull markets like the one we envision, P/E ratios rise along with investor optimism. It happened during the last two secular mega bull markets and we see no reason or argument that human nature won't again take the same course.

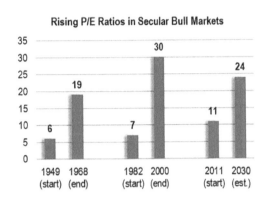

Rising P/E Ratios in Secular Bull Markets

During the last two secular bull markets the P/E ratio expanded by 3X (times) and 4X. Again being conservative, our estimate calls for only a 2X expansion in the P/E ratio.

From a different perspective, a P/E of 24 is historically very reasonable.

- For the past 25 years the average P/E was higher, 24.7. This is an average, which means it has been higher and lower.
- In every previous mega bull the P/E ratio has exceeded 24 numerous times.
- The 50 year average is 19.2, but it includes two secular bear markets and only one secular bull.

In reality, our projection of a P/E of 24 will probably turn out to be too conservative. A P/E of 30 would change the mega secular bull from one gaining 700% into one jumping 900%. Sound impossible? For perspective, the 1982-2000 secular bull gained over 1400%!

Putting the Data together for the Forecast

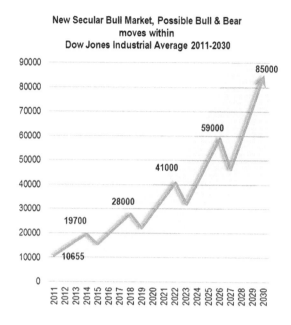

New Secular Bull Market, Possible Bull & Bear moves within Dow Jones Industrial Average 2011-2030

The start date of the new secular bull was **10/3/11**, the end of the last bear market in the secular bear market of 2000-11. The Dow was at 10655 and the S&P 500 closed at 1099. The length of the new mega bull is estimated to be 19 years, an average of the previous two secular bull markets, yielding **an estimated end date in 2030**.

Earnings will rise at an average of 7.2% over those 19 years for a **total gain of over 270%**. Applied to the S&P 500, this would give an earnings target of $363 in 2030.

Price/Earnings ratios will rise, and we are expecting the P/E ratio to double from a low of 11 in 2011 to at least **24 in 2030**.

Do the math to determine price:
Expected P/E ratio X expected earnings = price target
24 X $363 = 8712 for the S&P 500 for a gain of 700%.

A similar 700% gain for the Dow would be 10,655 + 74,585 (700% gain) = 85,240!!!!!!

If the new secular bull market is similar in pattern to prior ones, we could expect 5 cyclical bull market moves with an average gain of +85% over 3 years, and 4 cyclical bear markets with an average loss of -22% over 7 months.

In total, the new secular bull market will climb 700% over the coming decades. This could be conservative; while the 1949-68 secular bull rose 700%, the 1982-2000 vaulted higher by 1400% (S&P 500 Index).

SECOND MESSAGE

Aim Higher!!

- Be in the top 20% of investors.
- Do not settle for 700% in market returns.
- A 50% improvement in annualized return turns a 700% gain into a 2000% gain.
- Rare Opportunity, you can not afford to miss it.
- Do not buy and hope, be active.

Aim Higher

"The secret of success in life is to be ready for opportunity when it comes."

—Benjamin Disraeli

A new secular bull has started! Stocks will be moving higher! The Dow should exceed 85000!

Gains of 700% in the stock indexes will be common. You could stop reading, put down this book, buy a low cost index fund and enjoy the wealth headed your way. But we feel there is a smarter and wealthier alternative.

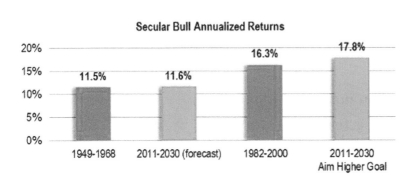

Our secular bull outlook calls for an annualized return of 11.6%. If that feels too optimistic, consider the fact that this return is 30% lower than the last secular bull markets (1982-00) annualized return of 16.3%. The projected 11.6% annualized return is almost identical to the 1949-68 secular bull market annualized return.

The Aim Higher goal is only slightly higher than the market's return during the 1982-00 secular bull, again within reach and not unrealistic.

Aim Higher

"11% or 17% in annualized return, what is the big deal? It's only 6% more, so why should I be so excited?"

Good question! Most of us think in terms of $'s, not in percentages. So let us look at the same chart of Secular Bull Returns from the previous page, but translated into dollars.

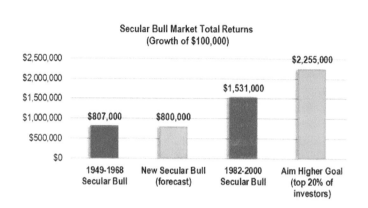

A big difference in total gains between the Aim Higher goal and the 1982-2000 period is not due to a higher return, but time. The 1982-2000 secular bull was +17 years, while the new secular bull is expected to last +19 years. Two additional years of gains can make a substantial difference.

This is a rare opportunity, so why settle for market average returns?

The market's 11.6% growth rate is a composite of the returns of different asset classes, sectors and industries. Some will be outperforming while others will underperform.

Our goal is to Aim Higher! Why settle for market returns, or just being average, when with some intelligence and effort you can be in the group of investors that will outperform?

Buying and holding a typical index fund will only achieve average returns. To achieve our Aim Higher returns you will need to be active.

Aim Higher

The Aim Higher goal of 17.8% will take some effort, but it can be reached. During the last secular bull (1982-2000) the average return was 16.3% but many mutual funds and indexes were able to beat that number by a wide margin.

The chart below reflects a shorter time frame of 12 years, however the annualized return for the S&P 500 Index is almost identical to the full secular bull.

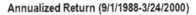

Annualized Return (9/1/1988-3/24/2000)

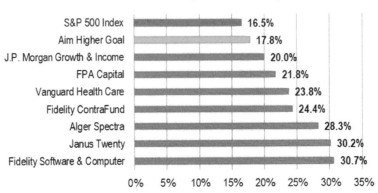

This is just a partial list; we chose names that you might be familiar with and funds with different investment styles. There is not just one way to outperform the market as this illustrates. In the coming chapters we will present four different active indexes that aim to outperform the market, striving to reach the Aim Higher goal.

Aim Higher! Time will be on your side!

Normally, investors view the market only in two dimensions: is it rising or falling? We believe that in reality it is three dimensional:

1. <u>Falling</u> with loss of capital.
2. <u>Rising and recovering the prior loss</u> of capital.
3. <u>Rising and creating new wealth</u>.

Falling markets cannot be entirely avoided, they happen. While losses can be mitigated with actively managed strategies and risk management (which we practice), the time spent in falling markets cannot. Rising markets carry two parts: time spent recovering from the losses and the most desired time, a rising market that is creating new wealth. (With risk management market losses should be minimized and therefore time spent recovering losses is shorter and more time is spent creating new wealth. These tables reflect the experience of a typical buy and hope investor without the benefit of risk management.)

With this perspective of time and market moves, **secular bull and bear markets are dramatically different.**

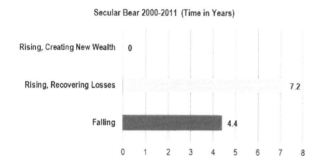

In the last Secular Bear market no time was devoted to creating new wealth. For a full 7 years the market was rising, but only recovering prior losses. The market spent 4 years falling. In total, over 11 years was spent riding a wild roller coaster that ended lower than it started.

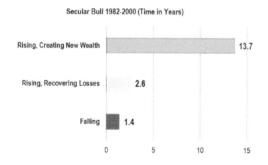

The story is just the *opposite in secular bulls;* the majority of the time is spent in <u>rising markets where new wealth is being created.</u> 14 years or 75% of the time in the last secular bull was spent creating new wealth, compared to 0% of the time in the secular bear.

Time is on our side in this new mega secular bull.
We need to use it wisely and profitably!!!

Aim Higher: Rare Opportunity

This is a rare opportunity. Secular bull markets only come around a few times in a century. Given this historical backdrop the following estimates the length of time for the current secular bull, when it may end, when the next secular bear will begin, and how long it will last before the cycle repeats itself. Obviously these are just estimates, but they are based upon historical precedence. While we may not know for a certainty when this mega secular bull ends, we do know for a certainty that if history means anything it will be followed by another secular bear (a lengthy period of no real returns).

A mega secular bull market has just started. For the majority of investors, if you miss this one, if you fail to take full advantage of this opportunity, the next secular bull will occur way past your peak investment years.

Age (2013)	Secular Bull 2011-2030	Next Secular Bear 2030-2045?	Next Secular Bull Start 2045?
25	25-42	42-57	57
35	35-52	52-67	67
40	40-57	57-72	72
50	50-67	67-77	77
60	60-77	77-87	87

The opportunity is today and will continue for the coming decades. Take advantage, do not miss out, participate, be active and Aim Higher.

Aim Higher!

"The biggest goal can be accomplished if you break it down into enough small steps."

—Henry Ford

To achieve top returns during this secular bull we need actively managed strategies that seek to achieve two goals:
- Over performance during the rising bull moves,
- With less risk during the declining bear moves.

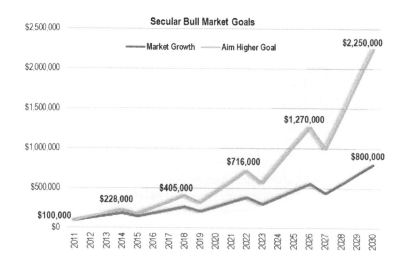

In the coming chapters we will be introducing several equity indexes (which can be made into strategies) where the research shows that these goals can be achieved in the past. Are these the only indexes that can accomplish the goals?

No. Many more exist, however, these indexes are several the authors are close to.

By explaining the active indexes, you will be able to see how to measure and what to look for in analyzing indexes or strategies.

Always consult with an experienced financial advisor on which strategies are appropriate for you based upon your investment time horizon and risk profile.

What is possible when the above goals are met during this mega secular bull market? The chart illustrates the potential if 1) during the projected bull market moves active management achieved a gain of 50% greater than the market, and 2) if during the inevitable declines, the losses (% decline) were no greater than the market.

If these incremental goals are achieved, instead of settling for a 700% market gain, the ultimate gain will be three times higher. The chart above illustrates the growth of $100,000 during the anticipated mega bull market: simple market gains turn $100,000 into $800,000. While achieving the Aim Higher goals, the same portfolio exceeds $2 million. In the coming chapters we will be measuring active indexes against these two goals.

Man's largest regrets in life are those opportunities which he did not commit to when he had the chance.

Aim Higher, what it can mean to you.

The graphs and mountain charts can be informative, but what is the potential for me?

You might be thinking, "I'm not starting with $100,000, my current balance is different. And I'm also making monthly contributions. So how can I make a comparison between my situation if I simply did nothing and enjoyed the expected market returns versus becoming more active and striving to reach the Aim Higher goals?"

Great questions. The following work sheet should help you determine the difference in the expectations of the two.

Lump Sum (your starting value today):

	Starting Value	5 Years	10 Years	15 Years	20 Years
11.6%: Market Returns	$100,000	$173,000	$300,000	$519,000	$900,000
17.8%: Aim Higher Goal	$100,000	$227,000	$515,000	$1,167,000	$2,650,000

	Annual Contributions	5 Years	10 Years	15 Years	20 Years
11.6%: Market Returns	$10,000	$64,800	$175,200	$366,400	$697,300
17.8%: Aim Higher Goal	$10,000	$74,700	$247,700	$617,200	$1,471,400

Please remember, the 11.6% in Market Returns and the 17.8% Aim Higher Goal are just <u>estimates and goals</u> of what could happen. What could or will happen will be different for every time period shown. Some years returns will fall short and actually show losses in comparison to the annualized expectations or forecasts. Other years will exceed either projection. The sole purpose of this exercise is to give you some expectation of the difference between anticipated market returns and what we hope can be accomplished with active indexes that are striving to outperform market returns (Aim Higher).

Figuring your Lump Sum Future Value

Step 1: Compare your current equity account balance to the $100,000 in the table above to determine what percentage you are starting with: for example, if your current account balance is $40,000 divided by $100,000 = 40% (your %).

$ _____ / $100,000 = _____ %

(Your current balance) (Your %)

Step 2: Then take your % and multiple it times the numbers appearing in the 'Lump Sum' table for both the market returns and the Aim Higher Goal for the time frame you have selected. Using the example above, the current account balance was 40% of the lump sum number. If the time frame you want to compare to was 15 years, you would multiply 40% x $519,000 (lump sum growth for market returns) which would equal $207.600. To determine the Aim Higher Goal, you would multiply the 40% x $1,167,000 (Aim Higher growth of $100,000) which would equal $466,800.

Market Returns   ___ % X $ _____ = $ _____
Aim Higher Goal   ___ % X $ _____ = $ _____

(Your %)   (Value for selected time period in table.)   (Estimated value.)

Figuring Potential Value of your Annual Contributions

$ _____ / $10,000 = _____ %

(Your annual Contributions) (Your %)

Step 3: Compare your current annual contributions to the $10,000 in the Annual Contribution table to determine what percentage you are: example, your current annual contributions are $7,000 divided by $10,000 = 70%.

Step 4: Then take your % and multiple it times the numbers appearing in the 'Annual Contribution' table for both the market returns and the Aim Higher Goal for the time frame you have selected. Using the example in **Step 3** above, the annual contribution was 70% of the lump sum number. If the time frame you want to compare to is 20 years, you would multiply 70% x $697,300 (growth of annual contribution with market returns) which would equal $488,100. To determine the Aim Higher Goal, you would multiply the 70% x $1,471,400 (growth of annual contributions with Aim Higher Goal) which would equal $1,030,000.

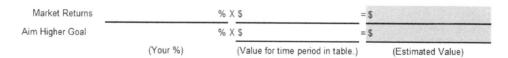

Market Returns   _____ % X $ _____ = $ _____
Aim Higher Goal   _____ % X $ _____ = $ _____

(Your %)   (Value for time period in table.)   (Estimated Value)

Total Potential value of Lump Sum and Annual Contributions

Step 5: Combine the answers from **Step 2** and **Step 4** to make the comparison for your situation.

	Market Returns	Aim Higher Goal
Lump Sum (Step 2)	$	$
Annual Contributions (Step 4)	$	$
Total Estimated Value	$	$

Given the analysis is correct, you could just buy a good low cost S&P 500 Index fund, sit back and earn market returns. Or you could Aim Higher, take full advantage of the current opportunity, become active and strive for significantly higher returns.

THIRD MESSAGE

Active Indexes

In the following chapters we will introduce several active indexes published by STIR Research LLC.

- Market Leaders Index
- Ultra Market Leaders Index
- Sector Growth Index
- Ultra Sector Index

The founders of STIR have over 5 decades of investment experience (see author's biography) in active allocation and research. STIR Research is a publisher of institutional research for advisors and institutional investors, not a broker/dealer or investment advisor and all research is non-personal.

Index performance is hypothetical because investors cannot invest directly into an index. Managed strategies, mutual funds, and ETFs have been developed by advisors and institutional investors to strive to mirror the performance of indexes. (Virtually every ETF is an attempt to mirror or track the performance of a given index).

As an example Vanguard and iShares provide emerging market ETFs and funds, but they are different as each is tracking a different index. The Vanguard fund strives to track an emerging market index which is published by the FTSE Group, an independent company which originated as a joint venture between the Financial Times and the London Stock Exchange. iShares emerging market ETF strives to mirror an index maintained by MSCI, formerly Morgan Stanley Capital International.

While managed accounts employing the strategies may closely track an index, there can be differences due to many factors, primarily transaction costs, available investment vehicles, trading restrictions, and advisory fees.

Dow 85000! Aim Higher!

Market Leaders Index

"Why buy the whole market when you can buy the market leaders?" Market Leaders strives to own the leading asset classes that can add to portfolio performance while avoiding lagging asset classes that can drain performance, and adjusting market exposure with changes in the trend and direction of the market.

To understand the potential of the Market Leaders Index, four concepts need to be explored.
1. Opportunities when Asset Classes perform differently,
2. Rotation and Identifying the Leaders,
3. The power in Persistency in Price and
4. Risk Management

Opportunities when Asset Classes perform differently: The "market" to which we often refer is not just a single entity; it can be broken down into separate investable parts (asset classes). And while the 'market' heads higher in the new secular bull gaining +700%, the individual parts (asset classes) will quite often behave significantly differently at different times, with some surging far ahead of the 'market' while others will lag. This difference in performance at various times provides investment opportunities for an active index.

The global market is full of opportunities and Market Leaders strives to capture the best of what the world offers. Market Leaders divides the global market into 8 distinct asset classes. Within the U.S, which makes up almost 50% of the world's equity market, it is divided into 6 asset classes, from large to small caps, and divided again by styles: value and growth. Internationally, developed countries like Japan and major European nations account for approximately 30% of global value, and Emerging Markets, like Brazil, China, India, represent the final 20%.

United States		International
Large Growth	Large Value	Developed Countries
Mid Cap Growth	Mid Cap Value	Emerging Markets
Small Cap Growth	Small Cap Growth	

Market Leaders Index

While the "market" is just an average of the performance of all the asset classes within in it, not all of the asset classes will perform the same at any given time. Over a quarter, a year, etc, there will be a big difference between the leading asset classes, the market average and the laggards.

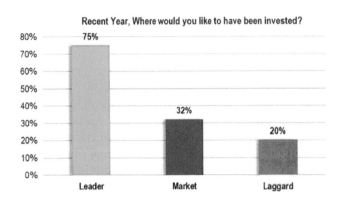

Recent Year, Where would you like to have been invested?

This example is typical, not that in the market goes up 32% per year, but the "spread" or difference between the leader and laggard asset classes is typically large. For the past decade, the spread between the two has ranged from a low of 17 percentage points to a high of 66! And therein lays the opportunity.

Unlike a fixed allocation, which will own all 8 of the 8 global asset classes, an active allocation will seek to gain a performance advantage by allocating its assets to the leaders while avoiding the laggards. The fixed allocation portfolio will ride the "market" up and down, going with the tide of the market. An active allocation seeks to identify the leaders and participate in their superior performance.

Numerous academic studies have determined that 80% to 90% of the performance of a portfolio will be determined by its asset allocation.

This makes sense, and that is why the Market Leaders Index strives to own the leading asset classes that can add to performance and avoid the laggards that can act as a drag on performance.

Market Leaders Index: How it Works

In addition to the large spread between the leaders and laggards, there is also a rotation between what is leading and lagging. In a given quarter or year or multiple years, what is leading in one, may not be next quarters or next year's leader.

Rotation Asset Classes

	Year 1	Year 2
Leader	Emerging Markets 75%	Small Growth 29%
Leader	Mid Growth 46%	Mid Growth 26%
Laggard	Small Value 21%	Large Value 20%
Laggard	Large Value 20%	Developed Countries 8%

Looking at this real life example, Emerging Markets was a leader one year, but not the second year becoming a laggard, (only two of the four laggards shown above). Mid Growth remained a leader. Small Growth was a laggard in Year 1, only to move up to a leader in Year 2.

So in addition to certain asset classes in any given year that provide over performance, rotation also exists between what leads in a certain time period and the next time period.

How do you identify what's leading and lagging? Fortunately there exists Persistency in Price, often referred to as momentum, or relative strength. What has been leading continues to lead and what has been lagging continues to lag.

Market Leaders Index, quarterly, looks back a set period of time, measuring momentum in price, and allocates among the equity asset classes within the index for the coming quarter: 40% to the #1 leader, 30% to #2 leading asset class, 20% to #3, and 10% to the 4th ranked asset class. It avoids the four poorest ranked asset classes, the laggards.

Market Leaders Index: How it Works

Market Leaders strives to own the leaders (asset classes) that can add to portfolio performance, while avoiding the laggards that can drain performance. This is active allocation; in contrast, a fixed allocation will own both the leaders and laggards, therefore having average performance. Obviously we want to do better.

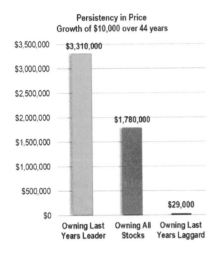

Persistency in Price
Growth of $10,000 over 44 years

Understanding there is rotation in the leadership, how can we identify the rotation when it occurs so that we can participate in the gains of the new leaders? Fortunately, there is "Persistency in Price" often referred to as "Relative Strength" or "Momentum": what is leading often continues to lead, and what is lagging often continues to lag.

Many Wall Street Maxims support the principle of "Persistency in Price": "Don't fight the tape," "Cut your losses and let your winners run" or "Make the trend your friend."

All these Wall Street maxims mean the same thing—— bet on price momentum.

Many studies, books, and articles have been written on this subject (Marshall did a presentation at the International Statistical Conference in Salt Lake City on this subject). But to illustrate the point, James P. O'Shaughnessy did one of the longest studies, which illustrates the power of Persistency in Price in his book "What Works on Wall Street".

Over a 44 year period, out of a universe of thousands of stocks, he built a portfolio of 50 stocks that were held for the coming year comprised of last year's leaders, and compared that return to a similar portfolio of 50 stocks comprised of the prior year's laggards.

If Persistency in Price works the leaders would continue to lead (building wealth) while the laggards would continue to lag (not where you want to have your money invested).

Results: a $10,000 investment in the Leaders grew to $3,300,000 versus the Laggard portfolio growing to $29,000!

Dow 85000! Aim Higher!

Market Leaders Index: How it Performs

However positive we are about this being a new mega rising market (secular bull), we are very aware that it will be interrupted by periods of falling prices (cyclical bear markets). Capital preservation is a key to success in an actively managed index. If you lose less of your hard-earned profits during the inevitable decline, you will have more capital to grow in the next rising market.

Market Losses	Gain Needed to Recover
-20%	25%
-30%	43%
-40%	67%
-50%	100%

As a recent example, during the horrific bear market of 2008-09, many fixed allocations fell by -50%. Therefore, the next bull market gain of +100% from 2009-2011 was essential just to get asset values back to where they were before the 2008 bear market began. Not only was it costly in money and lost time, but the roller coast ride was hard emotionally. Few investors stayed on the ride from beginning to end.

In contrast, an active index with risk management, strives to lose less during these inevitable market declines. If the loss had been contained at -20%, during the next 100% rally, only the first 25% of gains would have been needed to get you back to being whole. The remaining 75% of the advance would be spent earning new profits, not recouping old losses.

The Market Leaders Index, published by STIR Research, uses a risk management tool, the Market Environment Indicator (MEI), which measures the broad trend of the overall market. When this indicator is bullish, the Market Leaders research has the portfolio fully invested in the 4 leading asset classes. When the MEI is bearish (identifying a falling market), the Market Leaders portfolio equally reduces its equity exposure from 100% to 50%, with the 50% sold moved into the safety of money market or an Aggregate Bond index.

Market Leaders Index: How it Performs

The STIR Market Environment Indicator (MEI) strives to identify the <u>intermediate term</u> direction of the equity market. Weekly the MEI measures the trend and momentum of 100+ sectors and industry groups (S&P/MSCI Global Industry). Trend is a measurement of the direction of the sector or industry group's moving average. Momentum is the measurement of the rate of change (up or down) of the sector or industry groups price index.

By combining over 200 indicators measuring trend and momentum of underlying moving parts of the market, we believe MEI gives a more timely and accurate view of the market's direction and health than simply looking at one or two indicators. No indicator is perfect. It is impossible to sell consistently at the exact top or to buy at the exact bottom. A successful risk management indicator is one that:

- Is right more often than it is wrong.
- More importantly, when right it leads to participating in large gains (2009-2010) or avoiding large losses (like 2008), and when wrong, the losses usually are small and quickly reversed to being right.

In our opinion, the STIR Market Environment Indicator has proven to be a successful risk management tool. The MEI follows the old adage of "don't fight the tape"; it keeps us in trend with the market.

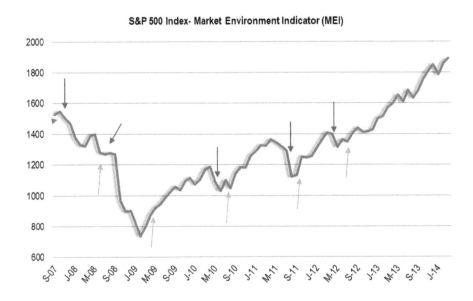

S&P 500 Index- Market Environment Indicator (MEI)

Market Leaders Index: How it Performs

The Aim Higher Goal has two parts:
1. Outperform the market during the bull market (rising prices) by 50%, and
2. During the market declines, lose less than the market.

Looking at the historical research, how does the Market Leaders Index measure up in rising markets? (Includes monthly data and only full cyclical bull and bear markets are shown)

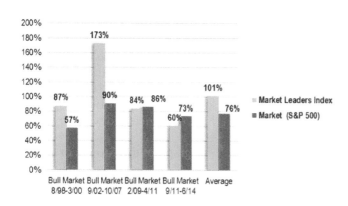

Looking at the past four bull markets, the Market Leaders Index's active allocation was able to outperform in two cases and matched the market's performance in two. In rising markets it was able on average to outperform the market by 35%.

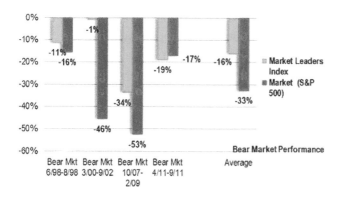

How does the Market Leaders Index perform during market declines?

In the period studied there were four bear markets; in three of the four Market Leaders risk management provided value by declining less, in only one case did it decline slightly more than the market. Overall, the average loss with Market Leaders in a down market was 50% less than the markets loss.

Market Leaders Index: Summary

The data indicates that the Market Leaders Index, with active allocation, almost matched the goal of outpacing market gains by 50% in rising bull markets and certainly did a better job on defense with the goal of not losing more than the market. But a casual observation would raise doubts. Because the Market Leaders Index wasn't able to meet the Aim Higher goals in every individual test, should it be rejected?

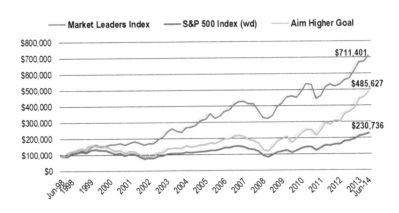

The graph illustrates the actual performance of the market over a 15 year period (6/98-9/13), a hypothetical example of meeting the Aim Higher goals of 50% better in bull markets and matching the market in bears (falling markets), and the performance of the Market Leaders Index.

The graph of the Growth of $100,000 tells a dramatically different story than a casual observation of the data.

- A stronger defense than the goal helped the overall performance.

- A strategy doesn't have to beat the market by 50% in every bull market to succeed in achieving the long term goal.

- The Aim Higher goal was $485,000, a gain of $385,000, significantly better than the $130,000 gain of the market.

- The Market Leaders Index value was over $711,000; the gain was over 60% higher than the Aim Higher goal's gain, and substantially better than the market's performance.

The Market Leaders Index from STIR Research uses only asset classes, and is reallocated quarterly. In the next chapter we will introduce a portfolio manager that will take the Market Leaders Index and turn it into an active strategy, striving to make it even better.

Turning an Index into a Strategy

The following is an interview with Troy Schield, of Disciplined Wealth Management (DWM). Working as a sub advisor to Flexible Plan Investments Ltd., a Bloomfield Hills, Michigan federally registered investment advisor created in 1981, DWM has incorporated several "upgrades" to the STIR Market Leaders Index research, striving to improve performance. Almost $500 million dollars has been invested in various Market Leaders strategies using the "advanced" methodologies developed by DWM & Flexible Plan Investments.

Question: It appears the Market Leaders Index works extremely well already. Is there really any way to improve upon that?

Troy: You are right; it is an impressive well diversified global core strategy. To achieve great levels of over performance you typically have to sacrifice diversification. I have seen many excellent active strategies that generate a lot of alpha (adding value over simple market returns), but almost all invest within a single asset class, like high yields, single sectors, etc.

Question: And why is that a problem?

Troy: It really isn't a problem, and there is a place for 'single' or 'focused 'asset class strategies in a portfolio. However, I prefer seeing an investment plan being built around a strong 'core' portfolio, which is well diversified over several asset classes before adding 'explore' strategies. It is a 'core and explore' approach.

Question: So how have you "advanced" the Market Leaders Index?

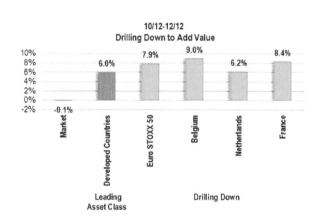

Troy: "The first way is 'drilling down' Let me give you an example. What I want to accomplish is to find the leading funds or ETF's within the leading asset classes. The concept is similar to the overall Market Leaders philosophy, some asset classes will outperform others, and likewise, some funds within the same asset class will outperform the asset class.

For example, recently, Developed Countries was a leading asset class, but 'drilling down' using relative strength analysis identified 5 leading country/region ETF's.

Turning an Index into a Strategy

Question: That is impressive! Were you "cherry picking," showing us the best?

Troy: No, history provides many of such examples, but I wanted to show how the concept of identifying the leading asset class adds on a level of performance and then how drilling down to the leading funds within that asset class can add another layer of value. That example illustrates the benefit of both.

During this time period, the U.S. stock market (S&P 500 Index) actually lost money, fractionally dropping -0.1%. The Market Leaders Index did its job and identified the leading asset classes, using persistency in price. Developed Countries gained 6% over the two months. Drilling down was able to add to that success, with the average of the four country specific ETF's selected from developed markets group of ETF's, gaining +7.8%. While an additional +1.8%, may not look that impressive, it's just one example, and here the 'drilling down' improved the performance by 30% over just owning the asset class.

Question: Does it always work that well?

Troy: I would hope so, but it doesn't. Obviously it works well over time because the drilling down follows the same success formula, persistency in price, in identifying the leading asset classes that adds value. But like picking leading asset classes it does not work every single time. Adding value often comes in small increments. Adding +1.8% on a portion of a four position portfolio over two months may not be impressive, however, over time it becomes a significant value added.

Turning an Index into a Strategy

Question: I notice in your example that the start date is November 1st, while the STIR Market Leaders Index reallocations start at the first of every quarter, which would have been October 1st. Is this the second 'advancement' you made?

Troy: Yes. While the STIR Market Leaders Index is reallocated to the top 4 asset classes at the beginning of every quarter, we do the reallocation analysis at the start of every new month. I believe it moves to new strength quicker. Below illustrates the difference in allocations during the 4th quarter of 2012.

Market Leaders 4th Quarter 2012 Allocation	ML Monthly Allocation October	ML Monthly Allocation November	ML Monthly Allocation December
Large Value	Large Value	Large Value	Developed Countries
Small Value	Small Value	Mid Value	Emerging Markets
Mid Value	Mid Value	Small Value	Large Value
Large Growth	Large Growth	Developed Countries	Mid Value

Notice that the monthly reallocation in October is identical to the STIR Market Leaders Index quarterly allocation. We both use the same relative strength/momentum analysis and therefore the first month of every new quarter will be the same. But in the next month, November, there were changes:
- Small Value and Mid Value traded rankings, small value fell to #3, and Mid Value rose to #2,
- Large Value remained the solid leader at #1, and therefore the largest allocation of the 4 leaders.
- The big change was that Large Growth dropped out and Developed Countries moved into #4.

In December the rankings again changed. Developed Countries moved to #1, Emerging Markets, a brand new allocation was added as #2, large value and mid value remained in the rankings but dropped in ranking.

What I want you to see is the big difference in the allocations in December for the monthly reallocated portfolio versus the STIR Market Leaders Index (1st box). With the monthly allocations the portfolio had moved a large allocation to internationals while no internationals were present in the quarterly allocation.

Turning an Index into a Strategy

Question: You have been working with this strategy for many years through bull and bear markets, what are some of the common misunderstanding of this strategy with brokers and advisors?

Troy: The most common misconception is incorrectly comparing Market Leaders to the wrong benchmark. It is an easy mistake. The Market Leaders Index is global. It looks at and can be invested domestically, internationally and in small and mid cap stocks. But the common benchmark used to make comparisons in performance is the S&P 500 Index. While that is a common benchmark, we need to remember that the S&P measures the performance of America's 500 leading companies. Because it is capitalization weighted, it is a reflection of the performance of just two asset classes: large growth and large value.

The performance of just domestic large caps can vary greatly from what is happening globally and even domestically. Making comparisons of a global strategy like Market leaders only to domestic large caps can lead to faulty conclusions.

Question: Can you give us an example?

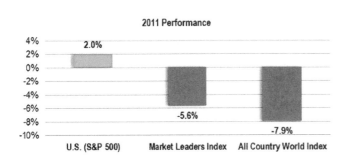

Troy: 2011. Everyone thought it was a bad relative performance year, and I'm using your Market Leaders Index numbers. The Index fell -5.6%, while the S&P 500 Index rose 2.0%; questions were asked, what went wrong? In fact, nothing went wrong. In reality Market Leaders actually outperformed the "market" by falling less.

A better benchmark is the All Country World Index (ACWI) which is global like Market Leaders. The composition of the ACWI is 47% U.S., 33% developed countries (Japan, United Kingdom, Germany, etc) and 20% emerging markets.

2011 was actually a good year for the Market Leaders Index on a relative basis, not a bad one as many have considered it. The Index did decline, but almost 30% less than the ACWI fall of -7.9%.

I realize that using the S&P 500 as the benchmark is almost the standard and has been for decades. However, as investors we no longer just invest at home. We look for opportunities abroad too. Therefore, we need to upgrade to a more inclusive index when making serious evaluations of relative performance.

Thank you.

Ultra Market Leaders Index

"A wise man will make more opportunities than he finds."

—Sir Francis Bacon

In a new secular mega bull market the investment winds will be at our back, pushing stock prices higher, much higher. This mega bull will present many opportunities.

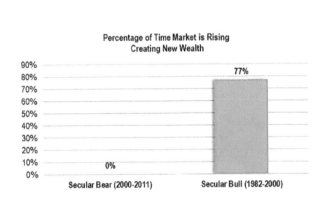

One of the great advantages of a new mega bull market is that the majority of the time will be spent creating new wealth. In the last secular bull market over 77% of the markets time was spent pushing into new high ground.

Translation: 77% of the time your portfolio was growing in value. It was working for you.

During a secular bear, the market does rise over 60% of the time, but that is all in an effort to make up for prior market losses with no real gains.

Secular bull markets are a breath of fresh air. New wealth is being created.

"Make hay while the sun is shining" is a great proverb and is certainly applicable to conditions today. Secular bull markets offer a rare opportunity and another way to magnify the potential gains is to employ Ultra ETF/funds.

Ultra Market Leaders Index

To reach the Aim Higher goals, we are striving for returns 50% greater than the markets in a rising environment. One way to make more of the opportunity is to judiciously use ultra funds to magnify returns.

What are ultra funds? They are leveraged index funds striving to achieve a daily return of twice (2X) the index they are tracking. As an example, the Russell 1000 Value Index fund (IWD), replicates the performance of large cap value stocks found within the largest 1000 companies in the U.S. Foe example, ProShares has created an index fund, the Ultra Russell 1000 Value Index fund, that strives to mirror the daily changes in IWD but by twice as much. Rydex and Direxion also offer these leveraged funds and ETF opportunities.

In concept, on rising days, the Ultra fund strives to double the performance on the upside of the underlying index it is tracking, and vice versa, on days with falling prices the losses for the Ultra fund should be twice as great as the underlying index.

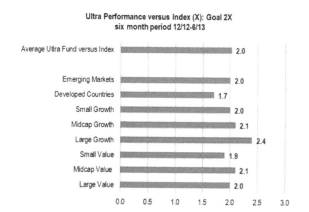

The ultra funds will not always exactly match a 2X move of the underlying index if held over long periods without periodic rebalancing but they do achieve their purpose of adding significant upside in rising markets.

Ultra Market Leaders Index: How it Works

Leverage can add great value or destroy value. Therefore leverage should be used with good judgment, implemented prudently only when market trends are favorable before taking action. Think of an experienced sailor choosing to employ a spinnaker for additional speed: The spinnaker fills with wind and balloons out in front of the boat when it is deployed, called *flying*. A spinnaker is only used in ideal weather, a great tool, but should never be used during adverse weather.

The same is here in the Ultra Market Leaders Index. Leverage like the spinnaker, should only be deployed under the most advantageous situations.

With the Market Leaders Index (using no leverage), it would be a mistake to take that index and to simply say "let's just replace the asset class index funds (1X) with ultra asset class index funds (2X)." You need to add leverage judiciously, only when conditions are most favorable.

Therefore we added another 'risk management' indicator to the Ultra Market Leaders Index, the Individual Fund signal (IFS). Each asset class often marches to a different drummer. The goal of an IFS signal is to identify the trend for an individual asset class. Also the math (quantitative analysis) behind each IFS can be quite different between asset classes. Truly, the IFS signal is tailored for each asset class. A Schield registered investment advisory firm was one of the first money managers to begin using the IFS back at the start of 1990.

Example: Emerging Markets over an 18 month period, using its tailored IFS.

The IFS generated a sell signal for Emerging Markets on 6/27/08 and remained bearish until 3/26/09.

Over that 9 month period Emerging Markets dropped 40% in value., something everyone would have wanted to avoid.

On March 26, 2009 the IFS generated a buy signal, and the Emerging Markets ETF (EEM) rose 60% over the final 9 months of 2009. This is a non-leverage fund.

Ultra Market Leaders Index: How it Works

The rules based Ultra Market Leaders Index combines decades of risk management experience. How do we combine the IFS (Individual Fund Signal) and MEI (Market Environment Indicator) to tell us the most opportune time to be invested (1X), or move to leverage (2X) or to be out of the asset class altogether and in the safety of cash? The answer is a two step process.

1. Look at the IFS on a daily basis to determine if the chosen asset class is on a buy or sell. If on a buy, take a 1X position in an index ETF or fund that corresponds to that asset class. Hold that position until the IFS indicates a change in trend. On a sell signal by the IFS, sell the ETF/fund and move the proceeds into a defensive position, either money market or aggregate bond.
2. Monitor the MEI on a weekly basis. When the MEI's trend and momentum is bullish, on an overall market buy signal, move all current buy recommendations in step 1 from a 1X into an ultra fund (2X) within that same asset class. If the MEI had been bullish (on a buy signal) and moves to a sell signal, immediately sell all ultra funds (2X) and move back to a 1X in the same asset class.

The IFS is the foundation that signals to the Index if the asset class should be bought or sold. The MEI only signals when it is okay to use leverage. If the MEI is bullish (on a buy signal) and the IFS is on a sell, the IFS is the overriding signal.

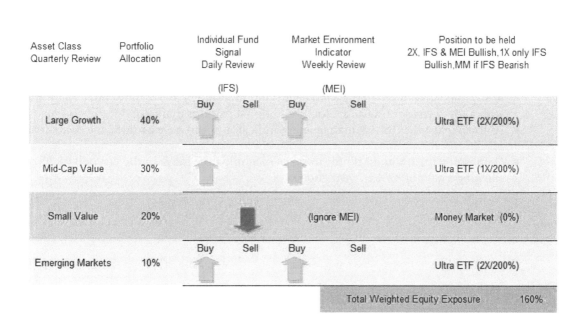

Ultra Market Leaders Index: How it Works

The chart of Emerging Markets (EEM) shows the rule set at work:

1. The IFS gave a sell on 6/27/08 at $40.79, moving the position defensively into cash.

2. The MEI turned briefly bullish (buy signal) in August, but with the IFS bearish, no action was needed or taken.

3. On 3/26/09 the IFS gave a buy signal for EEM at $24.30, at which time an index fund should be purchased (1X).

4. On 6/1/09 the MEI turned bullish and with the IFS bullish, following the rule set, the Emerging Markets Index fund (EEM) would be sold and replaced with the Leveraged Ultra Emerging (2x) Markets fund. Both the IFS and MEI remained bullish for the rest of 2009.

- The IFS kept the allocation out of harm's way (6/08-2/09) and avoided a -50% swan dive.
- The IFS signaled a change in direction with a buy signal on 3/26/09 and had the index participating in a great rally of +60% by year end.
- The MEI turned bullish in early June, giving the signal for clear sailing and therefore the go ahead to use leverage because the IFS was also bullish: that added another 22 percentage points in additional performance by year end, 82% versus 60%.
- A Buy and Hold of Emerging Markets would have shown a -5% move after 18 months, with a roller coaster ride and a lot of emotional pain for that loss.
- Following just the IFS risk management indicator would have avoided the swan dive and produced a 60% gain.
- Combining the IFS and MEI for leverage magnified the move in the last half of 2009, showing a gain of 82% by year end.

Ultra Market Leaders Index: How it Works

This rules based Index combines three levels of quantitative risk management analysis: relative strength, specific asset class trend and overall market direction.

Step One, Identify the Leading Asset Classes: Like the Market Leaders Index, quarterly 8 equity asset classes (represented in the All Country World Index) are ranked from leaders to laggards based upon relative strength/momentum analysis. Only the 4 leaders will make up the index for the coming quarter, with overweighting to the leader.

Step Two, Are the individual Leading Asset Classes in up trends or downtrends: Since 1990, the founders of STIR have implemented Individual Fund Signals (IFS) on a wide range of asset classes and sector ETF/funds. Each asset class has its own buy/sell signal which is monitored daily. A buy signal for the individual asset class directs a purchase with no leverage, and on a sell signal that asset class is sold, with the allocation going into a defensive position (money market or aggregate bond).

Step Three, employ leverage only if IFS is positive and Market Environment Indicator (MEI) is positive: the MEI is a measurement of the trend and momentum of the overall market. When the MEI is in an uptrend and confirmed with an uptrend in the IFS for a leading asset class, that asset class will takes a leveraged or 2X position.

The goal is an active index that judiciously employs the benefits of ultra ETF/funds at opportune times to enhance performance and with risk management.

Ultra Market Leaders Index: How it Performs

The Aim Higher Goal is broken into two parts:
1. Achieve a return 50% greater than the market during rising bull markets.
2. During the inevitable market declines, strive to lose less than the market.

Looking at the historical data, does the Ultra Markets Leader Index meet these goals? (Data is monthly and for the full cyclical bull and bear markets since 6/98)

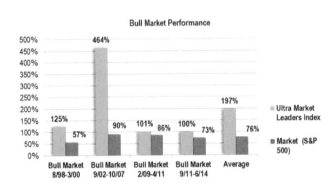

In each bull market the Ultra Market Leaders Index was able to outperform the broad market. The 5 year bull (9/02-10/07) pushed the average returns significantly higher. One could discount that as being a rarity, not to be repeated, but it also illustrates the potential during an extended time run (five years) while the other three bull markets lasted only 30 months or less.

Overall, the Ultra Market Leaders Index added significantly more than the goal of beating the market by 50%.

The second part of the Aim Higher Goal is not to lose more than the market, which is not an easy task when employing ultra funds. But that is why the rules based index utilizes two braking systems, the IFS and MEI.

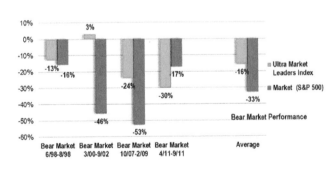

In 3 out of 4 bear markets the Ultra Market Leaders Index fell less than the market, and only during the brief and sharp 2011 bear market did it exceed the markets losses. In defense of the 2011 bear loss, the Ultra Market Leaders Index was +15% for the year prior to the 5-month bear decline, which takes some of the sting out of it.

Overall, the historically average decline met the Aim Higher Goal of smaller losses than the market.

Ultra Market Leaders Index: Summary

Active allocation worked: identifying the market's leading asset classes, followed up with individual trend analysis for buy and sell decisions and adding in leverage when the overall market was in an uptrend led to spectacular returns in the Index. Keep in mind that during this 15 year period, 11 years were mired in a secular bear market.

What led to the over performance?

- Asset class selection: instead of owning all the asset classes all the time (assuring that an investor will own the leaders and the laggards), the Ultra Market Leaders focused on the leaders that were able to add to portfolio performance.
- Risk Management: instead of riding the market down twice and suffering 50% losses, requiring 100% gains to get back to break even, the Ultra Market Leaders had a defensive strategy, a move out of equities.

Dow 85000! Aim Higher!

Sector Growth Index

This active index focuses on opportunities in sector funds. The broad market, like the S&P 500, can be sub-divided into ten smaller segments, called sectors, which group companies in similar lines of work. Investors use sectors to place investments into categories like technology, health care, energy, utilities and telecommunications. Each sector has unique characteristics and a different risk profile.

Putting company names with different sectors helps one visualize what a sector is:

- Technology is made up of companies like Apple, IBM, and Google.
- HealthCare contains Johnson & Johnson, Pfizer, Amgen, etc.
- Energy: Exxon, Schlumberger, Chevron and many others.
- Consumer Goods: Coca Cola, Procter & Gamble, Phillips Morris.

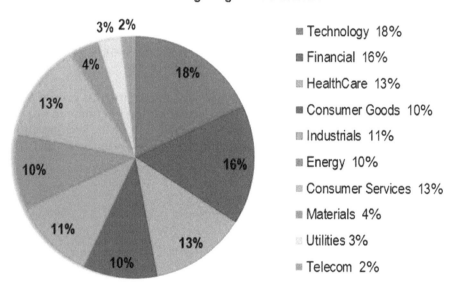

Sector Weightings in the Market

- Technology 18%
- Financial 16%
- HealthCare 13%
- Consumer Goods 10%
- Industrials 11%
- Energy 10%
- Consumer Services 13%
- Materials 4%
- Utilities 3%
- Telecom 2%

Sector Growth Index

While the economy and equity market can be divided into 10 sectors, each sector can be subdivided into smaller industry groups.

Technology Sector	Energy Sector	HealthCare Sector
Chips	Pipelines	Biotechnology
Computers	Refinery	Hospitals
Electronics	Drilling	Medical Supplies
Internet	Services	Pharmaceuticals
Software	Machinery	Medical Services

This is just a partial listing. As one example, S&P/MSCI produced a Global Industry Classification Standard (GICS) which consists of 10 sectors, 24 industry groups and 154 sub-industry groups. Investor's Business Daily follows its own classification system of 33 sectors and almost 200 industry groups.

Our goal here is to simply illustrate that another way of viewing the markets is to wear "sector/industry glasses."

The overall trend and performance of the broad market is the cumulative result of the trend and performance of the individual sectors. As the mega secular bull market marches to all time new highs, and accumulates even greater levels of wealth, so will each of the sectors, but not equally, and not in lock-step. And this is where the opportunity to outperform the market can be found by owning the leading growth sectors.

Sector Growth Index

The overall stock market performance is simply a roll-up of the performance of the 10 individual sectors. Some will outperform and others will underperform the broad market. As with the Market Leaders, there will be leading sectors and also lagging sectors. The following chart reflects some of the over and under performance by sectors/industry groups during the last full bull market.

The market gain of +102% for the S&P 500 is impressive and everyone would love to be part of that.

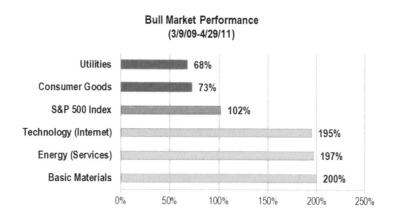

But not every sector performed equally. Some sectors lagged while others led. So why settle for average, owning the S&P 500?

The three sector/industry groups shown achieved returns almost two times greater than the market! While more defensive sectors, Utilities and Consumer Goods, underperformed.

The Aim Higher Goal of bull market returns greater than 50% than the markets is aggressive. To achieve that degree of over performance the advantage provided by being invested in the growth sectors/industry groups can be significant.

Sector Growth Index

Within the sectors, many are value oriented, like Utilities or Consumer Goods, while other sectors are considered growth, like Technology or Health Care. With our vision of a mega secular bull market in progress for the coming decades and wanting to Aim Higher, participating in the sectors with the greatest growth potential can boost returns further. There are 13 sector/industry groups the Sector Growth Index currently focuses on:

Health Care & Biotechnology: With an explosion of aging baby boomers over the next several decades the HealthCare sector is a natural choice. Another bright spot will be Biotechnology, with new medicines to improve healthcare, even eliminating some diseases and/or reducing some symptoms, therefore lowering long term costs.

Electronics, Internet, Telecom and Technology: Here are four growth/industry sectors. As the global economy expands so will the need for technology. Productivity growth, vital for corporate earnings expansion, is fueled by technology. We use new technology discoveries every day that no one dreamed of just a decade ago. The world now wakes up to iPhone communication, Amazon online buying, social networking on Facebook, Google internet searches and writing and computing with Microsoft software. New ideas will emerge that are beyond our imaginations.

Energy Services: We have highlighted technology advancements in the energy sector as one of the leading causes of the new secular bull market. It will grow as global demand increases. Some of the best investment opportunities are in the suppliers helping the industry; this is the modern day equivalent of selling shovels during the gold rush.

Basic Materials: As the world grows so does the demand for basic materials. As wealth increases, especially in emerging markets, demand for simple things we take for granted, like eggs, requires more fertilizer to improve grain production to feed more chickens. Growing economies require better infrastructures, leading to increased demand for more iron ore for steel, etc.

Retailing and Leisure: A growing economy means more jobs and higher disposable income, the driving forces behind consumer spending.

Financial Services and Banking: Expanding wealth leads to the need for increased financial services by individuals (retirement planning, savings, home loans, etc) and businesses (loans, lines of credit, new plants and equipment financing).

Real Estate: Baby boomers will be buying second homes and the Millennial's (a bigger generation than the Baby Boomers) will be forming new households and upgrading into new homes.

The Sector Growth Index focuses on the 13 growth sectors. It ignores the sectors which will see only modest growth, like utilities and consumer staples, which are more likely to be laggards than leaders.

Sector Growth Index

One of the goals of Aim Higher is to achieve a 50% greater return than the market when it is rising (bullish). With sectors we have the opportunity to divide the overall market into two parts: those leading sectors which over perform in rising markets and those that lag. Focusing on the over performing growth sectors improves the probabilities of reaching the 50% greater return in rising markets goal.

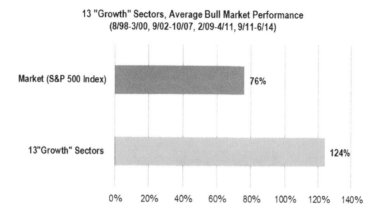

13 "Growth" Sectors, Average Bull Market Performance
(8/98-3/00, 9/02-10/07, 2/09-4/11, 9/11-6/14)

On average, during the last four bull markets, the 13 growth sectors outperformed the market by almost 65%!!

Knowing these 13 sectors historically have over performed, they become the investable universe for the Sector Growth Index.

Sector Growth Index

While on average each of the 13 growth sectors have outperformed during rising markets, that is not the case in every bull market. Individually, each of these 13 sectors can perform quite differently in rising markets. So <u>rotational investment opportunities</u> within the growth sectors occur and the Index strives to capture those higher gains.

Rotation in Sector Leadership

	Bull Market #1 (8/31/1998-3/31/2000)	Bull Market #2 (9/30/2002-10/31/2007)	Bull Market #3 (2/28/2009-4/29/2011)	Bull Market #4 (9/30/11-06/30/14)
Sector Leaders	Internet 702%	Energy Services 264%	Real Estate 213%	Biotechnology 161%
	Electronics 442%	Basic Materials 206%	Leisure 151%	Leisure 107%
	Biotechnology 299%	Real Estate 170%	Financial Services 135%	Internet 97%
Market	57%	90%	86%	73%
Sector Laggards	Leisure 37%	Electronics 85%	HealthCare 96%	Energy Services 69%
	Basic Materials 8%	Financial Services 82%	Biotechnology 75%	Telecom 35%
	Real Estate 5%	Banking 53%	Telecom 74%	Basic Materials 31%

The table reflects the changing leadership within the 13 growth sectors that make up the Sector Growth Index investable universe during the last 4 bull markets.

- In the 1998-2000 bull market Biotechnology rose almost 300% while Leisure gained only 37%. But in 2009-2011 Leisure powered ahead 150% while Biotechnology languished with just a 75% gain.
- Real Estate was a terrible laggard in the 1998-2000 bull run. Money invested here would have dragged down overall performance. It is a different story in the next two bull markets where in both cases the sector nearly doubled to almost tripled the market's gains!! Obviously at the time a leading sector to be invested in to add to performance.
- Not everything stays a consistent leader: Electronic was a star in the first bull market, but slightly lagged in the second.

So even after identifying the 13 leading growth sectors, we need to take the process one step further, identifying the current sector leaders throughout the current bull market.

Sector Growth Index: How it Works

STEP 1: Determining the Leading Sectors. Starting with a universe of 13 sector/industry groups, the index strives to own the 4 leading sectors/industry groups for the coming quarter. How to do that, relying on the time tested quantitative tool, <u>Persistency in Price</u>.

In the Market Leaders Index chapter we cited a study demonstrating how over a 44 year period, out of a universe of thousands of stocks, a portfolio of the previous year's leaders in price appreciation grew 3,300%. In comparison, the total gain of owning all the stocks gained just half as much, 1,770%. Picking the laggards in hope of a reversal was a disaster, with less than 200% gains. In our opinion <u>Persistency in Price works in identifying leaders.</u>

Below is an example of sector/industry rotation for the Sector Growth Index:

Q1 2013	Q2 2013	Q3 2013	Q4 2013	Q1 2014
Banking	Banking	Biotechnology	Biotechnology	Biotechnology
Financial Services	Financial Services	HealthCare	HealthCare	Technology
Internet	Internet	Retail	Internet	Internet
Basic Materials	Leisure	Leisure	Leisure	Leisure

Banking and Financial Services were leaders for the entire first half, gaining 19% and 20% respectively, versus an S&P 500 gain of +14%.

The Internet sector was also held for the first six months. In the 1st quarter it outperformed the S&P but lagged in the Q2. In total that position did add value by rising 11%.

For 2013, the Sector Growth Index had a mixture of winners with some that gained but did not lead. And this is probably what one should expect. But at the end of December, the Sector Growth Index had gained 40%, which was 33% more than the S&P's gain of 30%. And that is the type of over performance we are striving for.

Step 1 Summary: at the end of every quarter the index uses persistency in price to identify the four leading sectors/industry ETF/funds to be held equally for the coming quarter.

Sector Growth Index: How it Works

"Even being right 3 or 4 times out of 10 should yield a person a fortune,
if he has the sense to cut his losses quickly when he has been wrong."

—Bernard Baruch (financier, speculator, presidential adviser, 1870-1965)

STEP 2: Risk Management. Sectors that are more focused in their similar ownership are more sensitive to trends (profit, potential legislation, economic factors) in their sector than the trend and direction of the overall market. They are not immune to the trend of the overall market, but are more sensitive to what is happening at home. In essence, each sector can march to a different drummer.

As an example, a sharply rising trend in oil prices would be very beneficial for the energy sector and the energy services industry, but the same increase in oil prices could be a negative for the overall market.

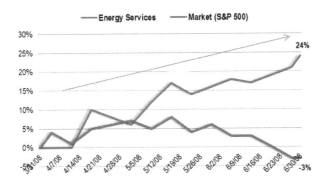

To properly manage risk when investing in sectors, you have to look at the trend of that sector, not the market. Since the early 1990's a Schield advisory firm was one of the first risk managers to practice "Individual Fund Signals" (IFS). The IFS is a mathematical (quantitative) signal tailored to each sector. The IFS is monitored daily.

A good example of a sector following its own drummer and not the market's was Energy Services during the second quarter of 2008.

Energy Services had passed Step 1; it was identified as one of the leading sectors.

The Individual Fund Signal for Energy Services was in an uptrend and therefore on a buy signal.

The overall market was in a sharply falling bear market. The Market Environment Indicator was negative.

By following the IFS buy a(4/4/08) energy services contributed a positive return of 24% (1/4th of the index) while the market lost 3%.

The Sector Growth Index can move from 100% invested to 0% equity allocation in 25% increments depending upon the sectors individual fund signal. When a leading sector's IFS is on a sell, that 25% allocation to the index is moved to a defensive position, either money markets or aggregate bond.

Sector Growth Index: How it performs

Rule Based: Starting with a universe of 13 growth sector/industry groups, on a quarterly basis utilizing persistency in price to identify the four leading sectors for the coming quarter (rule #1) combined with the IFS for risk management (rule #2), the Sector Growth Index strives to own the leading sectors in uptrends.

The first part of the Aim Higher goal is to outperform the market in rising periods by 50%. In the cyclical bull market within a secular bull, 8/1998-3/2000, the Sector Growth Index did 3X better, however in the most recent bull (9/11-3/14) it matched the market move.

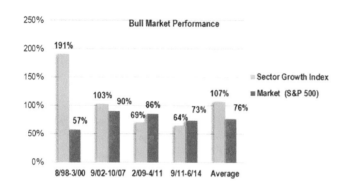

But during the cyclical bulls within a secular bear, the Index outperformed once and slightly lagged during the 2nd.

With the market in a new mega bull market, we would expect the Sector Growth Index to exhibit more of the over performance as seen in the cyclical bull during a secular bull.

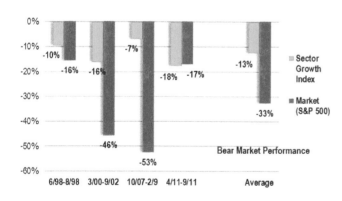

During the inevitable market declines, the Sector Growth Index did significantly better than the market by declining less. In only one case, the 4/2011-9/2011 quick bear market, did the Index give up more than the market.

The Individual Fund Signals did their job, and kept the Sector Growth Index out of major trouble, especially when the market was falling -46% and -53%.

Overall the average loss in the Sector Growth Index during bear markets was almost 60% less than the market's decline. Looking forward and at history, cyclical bear markets within a secular bull tend to be both short in duration and shallow (smaller) than seen during a secular bear. Therefore, future bear markets, which will occur, will likely be similar to 6/1998-8/1998 or 4/2011-9/2011.

Aim Higher: Sector Growth Index Summary

+830% gain for the Sector Growth Index versus a market advance of +120%.

Instead of owning all of the sectors all of the time (which the benchmark index S&P 500 does), the Sector Growth Index strives to own the leading sectors in up trends. History shows this to be a more rewarding investment strategy.

Active allocation can add tremendous value both by increasing returns in rising markets and reducing losses in falling markets.

The long term Aim Higher Goal is to grow 3X or +2100% versus the forecast of 700% for the market during this new mega bull market over the coming two decades. While past performance is never a guarantee of future performance, outperforming the market (S&P 500 Index without dividends, 73%) by 12X over the past 15 years, gives us comfort that a 3X goal is achievable.

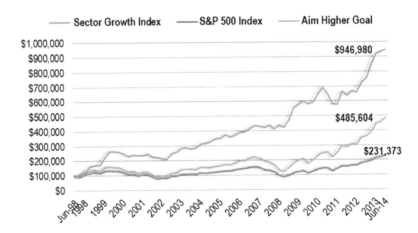

Ultra Sector Index

"Spend eighty percent of your time focusing on the opportunities of tomorrow rather than the problems of yesterday."

—Brian Tracy

If this mega bull is anything like the last one (1982-2000) investors could expect that over 92% of the time the market will be rallying (creating new wealth 77% of the time, and recovering losses 15% of the time). So let us follow the advice of Brian Tracy and focus on the opportunities of tomorrow.

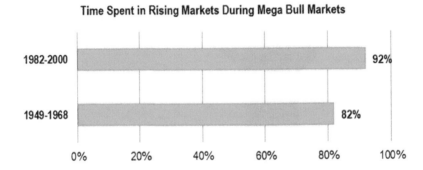

Time Spent in Rising Markets During Mega Bull Markets

Was the time spent rising from 1982-2000 of 92% a fluke? No. Taking a look at the mega bull market of 1949 through 1968, 19½ years, the time spent in a rising market is also significant, 82%.

Mega secular bull markets represent a rare opportunity for investors. We need to take full advantage of them when they occur. Investors need to grasp this time with both hands and focus on reaping the highest returns possible within their risk tolerance.

As demonstrated in the Ultra Market Leaders Index, one methodology for reaping higher returns is to judiciously employ ultra funds.

Ultra Sector Index

Ultra funds strive to duplicate twice (2X) the daily move within the underlying index they are tracking. Some ultra funds are designed for 3X moves (three times the daily % change in the underlying index), but within the Ultra Sector and Ultra Market Leaders Indexes only 2X ultra funds are utilized.

The key phrase in ultra funds is <u>to strive to duplicate twice the daily move.</u> While the ultra funds typically come close, when held for long periods without frequent rebalancing the result is not always exactly two times the move in the underlying index.

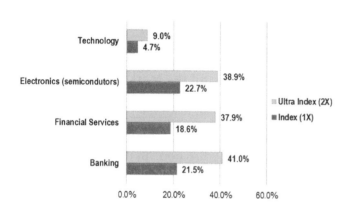

Ultra Banking was impressive with a 41% gain, but that was just 1.9X the underlying index. And Ultra Technology also came in at 1.9X.

Only the Ultra Financial Services ETF was able to hit the 2X goal.

The ultra funds did meet the goal of significantly higher returns than the benchmark index, but not always an exact 2X move of the underlying index.

Ultra Sector Index: How it Works

Tracking the Market Leaders Index as a foundation and only adding ultra funds at the opportune time proved to be successful when applied to the Ultra Market Leaders Index. The Ultra Sector Index follows the same formula, using the Sector Growth Index as its foundation.

Step 1, Identify the Leading Sectors: Using the predictive power of persistency in price, on a quarterly basis rank the 13 growth sectors, identifying the 4 leaders to be included equally within the index and avoiding the other nine.

Step 2, Determine on an Individual Basis if the Leading Sectors are in Up Trends or Down Trends: applying the Individual Fund Signal (IFS) developed specifically for that sector, determines if the sector is on a buy signal, and therefore is to be included in the index, or if it is on a sell signal, puts that 25% allocation into a defensive money market or bond position.

Step 3: Use Leverage (2X) only if the IFS Signal is Positive and the Market Environment Indicator (MEI) is also Positive. The index is striving to put the probabilities of success in its favor by using two independent signals to verify the most opportune time for leverage.

The Ultra Sector Index is active and rules based and can range from 200% to 0% equity exposure (and in between) based upon individual sector trends and overall market direction. In the example below, 3 of the leading sectors had a rising/bullish IFS and with the MEI bullish, were placed in ultra funds with 2X leverage. One position's IFS was falling/bearish and therefore was moved to money market or aggregate bonds. The IFS takes precedence over the MEI. Therefore the resulting overall index was only at a 150% invested position.

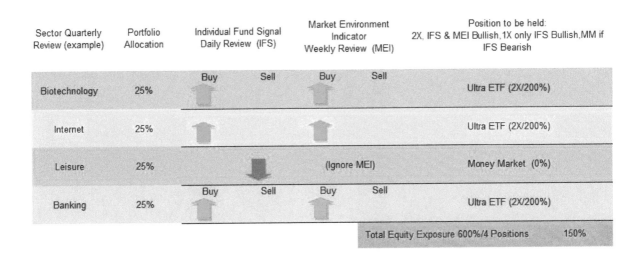

Ultra Sector Index: How it Performs

Looking at the past four full bull markets, the Ultra Sector Index outperformed in each case.

The 8/1998-3/2000 was an unusual period of time and that should be taken into account. Quite often at the end of massive bull runs, like from 1982-2000, individual stocks and markets can have a "blow off top." Final moves can be extremely large and rarely repeated as we saw when internet stocks rose over 700% during that period.

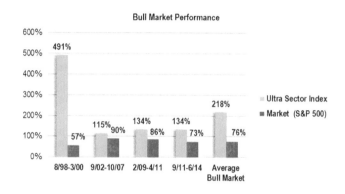

Looking at the two bull markets, both occurring within a longer term secular bear market, the Ultra Sector Index was able to outperform the broad market by over 40%.

Another observation. <u>During cyclical bull markets within secular bull markets</u>, like 8/1998-3/2000 and 9/11-6/14, optimism is running high and quite often one or two sectors will break out and have significant moves driving overall performance higher. But within a <u>cyclical bull market in a secular bear market</u>, when investors are more pessimistic than optimistic, large breakouts in leading sectors are rarer, therefore relative over performance is muted. While one should not expect or count on +500% gains over a short period of time (a repeat of 8/1998-3/2000), one could anticipate higher relative performance during an ongoing lengthy secular bull market.

Ultra Sector Index: How it Performs

Overall, the Ultra Sector Index performance during falling markets was impressive for an index that can be leveraged. Normal expectations would be that losses from a leveraged index would run significantly higher than the overall market.

So why did that not occur?

Two different risk management styles or 'braking' systems are employed.

From 6/1998 to 8/1998 the MEI turned bearish and leverage was removed after the market had declined only -4%, before eventually falling -16%.

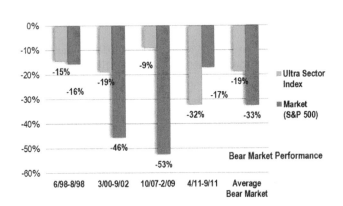

During 3/2000 to 9/2002 bear market, the markets horrific losses didn't all occur at the start but in 2001 and 2002 when again the MEI had already turned bearish, there was no leverage in the index, and most of the leading sectors IFS were on sells so the index was entirely out of the market during the hardest hit period.

The MEI turned bearish on 11/5/2007 early in the bear market 10/2007-2/2009 and again all leverage was removed for the entire bear market, with the brief exception of a three week period in 2008. During the worst period, 9/2008-2/2009 when the S&P fell -38%, the majority of the time the Individual Fund Signals were also on sells, therefore the index was almost 100% in a defensive position in bond funds, which gained 4%.

During the 4/11-9/11 bear market, the Ultra Sector Index under performed by a wide margin. The bear market drop was quick and sharp. The MEI, which is trend following the broad market, did not turn bearish until early August, after the majority of the damage of the bear market had occurred. Fortunately the IFS signals had turned negative prior to that time, but not before large losses occurred. The only bright spot, the Index had gained 21% early in 2011 before the quick five month bear market began, taking some of the pain out of the decline.

Ultra Sector Index

Nothing is perfect: Even by employing two risk management strategies losses will occur. In 2011, a year with a global bear market mid year, all 4 sectors gave up ground. The Ultra Sector Index lost 19.5% for the year. Losses should be expected.

Two goals to keep in mind with risk management tools:

1. <u>They will be right more often than wrong</u>. But again, there will be times the signals will be wrong: the index will be buying when in hindsight it should not have. At other times, a sell signal will occur, but the sector keeps rising in price and the index misses out on some of an investment opportunity. Signals can be wrong several times in a row. That will be discouraging.

2. <u>And more important than #1, when right, the gains can be bigger or the avoided losses can be larger,</u> and when wrong, the missed buying opportunities can be small or the losses can be minimal.

Historically, both the STIR Market Environment Indicator and the Individual Fund Signals have met these goals. But past performance is no guarantee of future performance. Good advice. That is why both risk management tools are constantly evaluated.

Ultra Sector Index: Summary

A 2,800% gain over plus 16 years versus a market advance of 130% is impressive. However, an initial bull market advance of 491% had a big influence on that large advance. Looking at more recent periods, from the lows of 2011 through new highs in June, 2014 the market advanced 73% and the Ultra Sector Index did 84% better with a 134% gain.

The Dow 85000 forecast is for a 700% mega bull market gain by 2030 or 11.6% annualized return. The Aim Higher Goal seeks an annualized return of 17.8% or 50% greater for a total gain of 2,100% (3X) over 17 years.

- For the past 10 years the Ultra Sector Index grew at an annualized rate of 18.1%, over three times (3X) the S&P 500's annualized gain of 5.6% (6/2004-6/2014).

- For the past 5 year period, the market had a 16.3% annualized gain, compared to the Ultra Sector 26.4% annualized gain, again performing 50% better than the market (6/2009-6/2014).

The Ultra Sector Index, even during a secular bear market was able to meet the Aim Higher annualized return goal for the majority of the time. Chances are during a secular bull market, where the market spends more time rising, the Ultra Sector Index will continue to meet the Aim Higher goal.

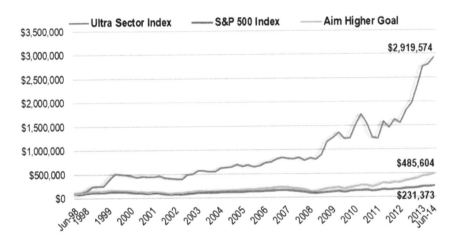

Turning the Sector Indexes into Strategies

This is the second interview with Troy Schield, Disciplined Wealth Management (DWM), his insights on the Sector Growth Index and Ultra Sector Index.

Question: You have been doing security analysis for over 25 years, equity or bond asset classes and sectors. What role do sectors play in an overall investment plan?

Troy: I'm an active manger. I'm always looking for ways to add higher returns with less risk. The leading sector funds historically offer the potential of higher returns than the leading asset classes because they are more focused while asset classes are more broadly diversified. Sectors also play an important role in expanding investment options, a great addition to a core portfolio.

Question: How about a quick example of the higher relative returns?

Troy: Take 2013, a big year for the domestic market, domestic asset classes (like those in Market Leaders) and sectors. It was a tough year to add excess return when the S&P 500 gained 30%, leading virtually all the world indexes (the All Country World Index ex US had half the gains or the S&P, up just 15%). However, look at the performance of the two leading sectors compared to the two leading asset classes and you can see the potential of sectors.

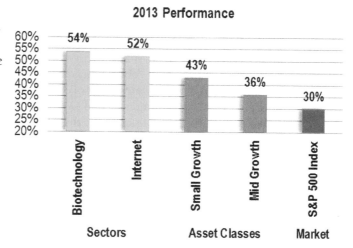

The two sectors outperfomed the market by 75% while the two asset classes, still doing great, outperformed by 31%.

Question: I see the potential however you mentioned seeking higher returns with less risk. Sectors, being industry specific, are more volatile, your thoughts on risk management?

Troy: This is where I started with sectors, risk management. Some twenty plus years ago advisors would bring the firm (Schield Management Company) accounts that were invested in single sectors, like technology, precious metals, etc. I was responsible for developing the quantitative buy and sell signals for each of the different sectors. And I see you retained the name Individual Fund Signal. Because each sector can move differently than the overall market on occasion, an overall market signal isn't always ideal. Each sector marches to a different tune and therefore a different mathematical signal is essential for risk management.

Question: So what tweaks have you applied to the Sector Growth Index? It has exceeded the Aim Higher goal, so where did you see additional opportunities?

Troy: In Market Leaders I was able to 'drill down' to the leading funds within the leading asset class, that isn't a realistic alternative with sectors. The sectors are already focused and specific, it is hard to find large differences between one financial service sector fund and another, as an example.

However, I do see an opportunity for enhancing the returns by moving to a monthly versus a quarterly reallocation (like in the Market Leaders Index) to the leading sectors. Sectors tend to move quicker and leadership can often change within a 90 day period, thereby creating an investment opportunity by moving to strength quicker.

Sector Allocations	Jan-13	Feb-13	Mar-13
	Banking	Banking	Banking
	Internet	Internet	Internet
	Financial Services	Financial Services	Financial Services
	Basic Materials	Leisure	Leisure

The first quarter of 2013 is one example: both the quarterly and monthly reallocations will be the same during the first month of every new quarter. Only during the second and third month of the quarter could differences in leadership occur.

Quite often any change between quarterly and monthly reallocation might occur in just in one or two sectors. Using the monthly reallocation, in February leadership remained identical in three sectors with the exception Leisure replaced Basic Materials for February and again in March. Over that two month period Leisure gained 7.8% versus a decline of -2.3% for Basic Materials. While this single change only represented 25% of the overall portfolio, the other 75% remained unchanged, the monthly reallocation added 2.5% gain to the overall portfolio's performance versus the quarterly reallocation during the first quarter.

Question: Does it always work that well?

Troy: Not always. As you see in the example that by going the extra mile with a monthly move to strength, that quite often the change in the sector portfolio is rather small. Where I see the larger potential benefit is at turning points or major inflection points. At market tops in 2007 and 2011 or bottoms like in 2009 and 2011, leadership can change quickly and therefore by looking at a monthly analysis will identify new sector leadership quicker.

Question: What ideas did you see with the Ultra Sector Index? It had to be a challenge to improve upon an index with two sets of brakes and the potential of 2X gains in a rising market.

Troy: Your right, the Ultra Sector is impressive in construction. Being raised on risk management I loved the concept of integrating two time tested risk management systems into a single index. As I mentioned earlier, I began working with Individual Fund Signals some 25 years ago and know first-hand its rewards and pitfalls. My history with the Market Environment Indicator is over a decade and I watched it work beautifully. It stayed with the upward trend during the bull markets and avoiding the majority of the 2007-2009 bear market, impressive.

The sector universe could be larger, however, within a long term secular bull market like the book is forecasting it only makes sense to stick with a universe of sectors that have demonstrated superior performance in the past. So I really don't see any changes there, but always be open to add a sector fund/ETF when new ones are created.

Question: So no ideas?

Troy: Oh, I have a couple. I would approach an ultra sector model with two changes, which fit my conservative personality better.

First, using ultra funds with their greater volatility, I would certainly want to move to monthly reallocations with that additional speed to move to strength sooner.

Second, my comfort level is higher using 1.5X ultra funds versus 2X. [A 1.5X fund strives to match a 150% of the daily move of the underlying index]. Granted, in big years like 2013 a 1.5X portfolio will simply not keep up with the 2X on the upside. However, during those inevitable down years, like 2011 where the drops are quick and sharp, even with two levels of risk management, the potential drawdown's will be much smaller with 1.5X sector funds than the 2X funds. It is my experience that clients would often choose smaller losses even if they give up some of the potential on the upside.

Hopefully, by combining the monthly reallocations, which strives to add value over the quarterly analysis, and giving up a little on the upside with the lower volatile 1.5X funds but with smaller drawdown's, that this combination could still deliver a return that would give the Ultra Sector Index a good run for its money.

Question: Sounds like a challenge?

Troy: One of my favorite quotes is from Warren Buffett, "We don't have to be smarter than the rest. We have to be more disciplined than the rest."

Discipline, especially in investing, is hard to practice all the time. Different market environments will challenge your discipline. That is why I'm a big believer in combining strategies for a smoother investment experience, less risk and long term an overall investment plan where the investor will have the discipline to stick with.

I love football, especially watching my home team the Broncos. Some games our quarterback, Peyton Manning, is on fire and setting records, other games the defense is sacking and creating all sorts of havoc, and other days the special teams will score with a kickoff return. My point is it is a team effort that takes football franchise to the playoffs and a shot at the Super Bowl.

That is what you want in an investment plan, a great team that will take you to your goals. A great investment team is made up of Market Leaders, with the ability to invest internationally and drill down to leading funds within leading asset classes, balanced out with sectors that in the right market climate can over deliver. A good balance leads to a smoother ride helping investors with their discipline.

Question: Great analogy, any examples of 'team' strength?

Troy: Sure, take the great five year bull market run from 9/02-10/07 where the S&P 500 rose an impressive 90%. Looking at the Sector Growth Index it struggled during that time to outperform. On an annual basis was only able to beat the benchmark 50% of the time. That could test ones discipline. While the sectors ended the five year bull market with a 103% gain, beating the 90% move in the S&P 500 it was a struggle.

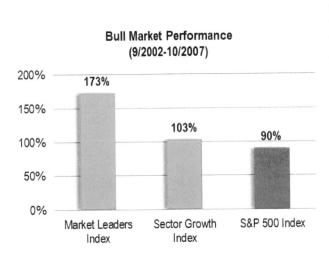

In comparison, the Market Leaders Index was a powerhouse, gaining 173%, almost twice the gain of the overall market. Why, internationals (Developed Countries and Emerging Markets). Emerging Markets played a big role in those gains. Plus, not shown in the index, the ability to drill down to leading funds could have possibly added even more value. A pure sector rotation lacks that international element that is why it should be used as a supplement to Market Leaders in building a stronger team.

Question: At other times the team is winning because of the strength in sectors, correct?

Troy: Yes. In other years, a good exposure to sectors will be what is winning. In 2013 it was a tough year to outperform possibly the best performing market in the world, the S&P 500 Index. However, the Sector Growth Index did just that, moving 40% higher. The Market Leaders Index came in with a respectable 26% move.

If all you owned was the Market Leaders your discipline might have been tested. But with broader exposure to sectors, that excess return would have given you a higher return and therefore making it easier to stick with your discipline.

Question: Any last words of wisdom?

Troy: Many will look at 2013 and see the 50% gain in the Ultra Market Leaders Index or the 76% move in Ultra Sector Index or the 40% jump in the Sector Growth Index and say 'wow, that was great but probably not going to happen again'. That will be a mistake. Big years may be more normal than one might think.

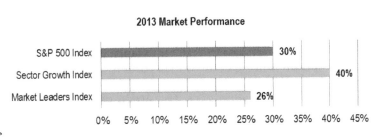

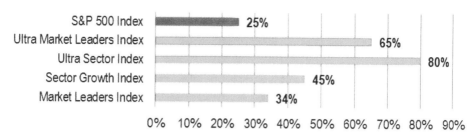

**Average Index Performance
When the S&P 500 Gained +20% in a Year (12/98-12/13)**

S&P 500 Index — 25%
Ultra Market Leaders Index — 65%
Ultra Sector Index — 80%
Sector Growth Index — 45%
Market Leaders Index — 34%

Secular bulls are very different than secular bears in many ways that few understand. Your book does a good job of explaining the long term potential but drill down and take a look at the differences of what you might expect every year:

- 20%+ annual moves occur only about 15% of the time in secular bears,
- While gains of over 20% occurred 40% of the time during the secular bull of 1982-2000.

In secular bulls, 20%+ moves like in 2013 could be occurring quite often and if you are aiming higher you need to really capitalize on those opportunities.

Question: Great point, looking at all the years of 20+% gains in the market, the Sector Growth, Ultra Sector and Ultra Market Leaders really did live up to their Aim Higher goals. Any final comments?

Troy: Yes, experience and expertise, a little bit of follow up on my last comments. Too many investors and advisors still live with a bear mentality. They put too much judgment of expertise on how well a strategy or index did during the last major bear market, typically 2008-9 and to a certain point that is fine. The two sector indexes gave up very little ground while avoiding the disastrous market loss of 53%. Really not hard to do when almost every trend was straight down.

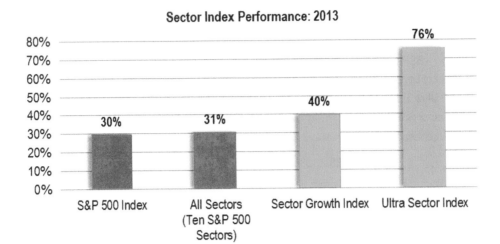

Sector Index Performance: 2013

However, in a secular bull the declines will be shallow and short and the <u>real test of expertise will be measured on how well you do on the upside</u>. When you get those great 20%+ up years and there will be many of them, will a sector strategy have the expertise to really excel? To excel you will have to be selective, owning the leading sectors. 2013 is a great example.

A sector strategy that ends up buying all the sectors will just give you market returns.

The Sector Growth Index and Ultra Sector Index reallocate to the leading sectors, thus the superior performance. I believe and hope that 2013 isn't just a one year wonder but we will see multiple repeats during this secular bull!

Thank you.

Turning an Index into a Strategy

The Sector Growth Index and Ultra Sector Index measure the value of a rule based active risk managed sector rotation. That may sound complex, but hopefully the previous pages have walked you through the rules of how each of the sector indexes are constructed. All indexes are mathematically constructed and may not be invested in directly. But many strategies, mutual funds and ETF's attempt to 'track' an index. The following interviews are with experienced 'active' money managers, who have, like with the Market Leaders Index, incorporated 'upgrades' to the indexing process, striving to improve performance.

Jerry Wagner is the President of Flexible Plan Investments, Ltd. since its formation in February 1981. He has been active in market analysis, designing methodologies and management of personal investment portfolios since 1969 and currently manages almost $2 billion in assets for thousands of clients. By careful and intelligent risk management, his firm's clients safely avoided the down market of 1984, the devastating crash of 1987 and the 1990 sell offs. Clients using Flexible Plan's approach to strategic diversification ameliorated the impact of investment losses as experienced by various market indexes in the "mauling" of this recent bear markets. Flexible Plan's success has been highlighted in important trade publications such as Business Week, Barron's and Mutual Funds Magazine, and has been repeatedly listed among the Inc. Magazine's 500 Fastest-Growing Private Companies.

Question: Jerry, thank you for taking the time and applying your extensive knowledge and experience in reviewing the Sector Growth Index and Ultra Sector Index.

Jerry: Thank you for the compliments, I always love looking at innovative active market ideas. I was glad to see the addition of several sector rotations ideas, sort of a follow up on your book "Sector Funds for Trophy Returns', which I enjoyed also.

Question: Thank you, but with your great analytical mind and having reviewed hundreds of market indexes and strategies, do you have any initial observations?

Jerry: One that pops out first is by restricting the sector universe to 'growth sectors' based upon past performance are the indexes guilty of selective or 'selection' bias?

Question: Great question, but for the readers, can you explain in more depth what 'selection' bias is?

Jerry: Selection bias is really a statistical bias in which the researcher "cherry picks" or chooses with the benefit of hindsight the components of an index. If there is selection bias then the research may be flawed.

Basically, is the over performance of both the sector indexes over the market simply due to choosing the best performing sectors in the past to make up the 'growth' sector universe and in that selection process eliminating the laggards that would drag down performance? Or is the over performance a reflection of the actual value being added through the active rules (quarterly selection process, individual fund signals and using the Market Environment Indicator for adding leverage)?

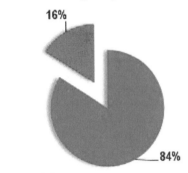

Sector Weightings in the Market

16%

84%

■ Growth' Sectors

■ Excluded Sectors: Utilities & Consumer Staples

Authors' response: Looking at the major sectors that make up the market, the sector indexes include 86% of all sectors. The 'growth' sector universe excludes Utilities, which makes up 4% of the entire market and Consumer Staples, which accounts for another 12%. By focusing the rotational analysis on 13 different sectors and industries, I believe the indexes have a broad exposure to the majority of the market.

So from a 'selection' bias perspective, the indexes do include the vast majority of the sectors that make up the market.

Jerry: That eliminates part of the concern on selection bias; it does appear that by including 84% of all of the sectors that the universe is very inclusive.

But it doesn't entirely resolve my question. With the elimination of Utilities and Consumer Products over the 16 year period (6/98-3/14), do you think that may have led to over stating the positive returns of the sector indexs? Have you looked at that?

Authors' response: It is possible that the elimination of Utilities and Consumer Products over the 16 year period may have actually lowered the potential returns of the sector indexes. Both sectors outperformed the market, with consumer staples almost gaining twice as much. Source FastTrack: Utilities (FSUTX), Consumer Staples (FDFAX), S&P 500 (sp-cp)

Jerry: That clears up the question of 'selection' bias accounting for the over performance of the sector indexes, it appears it didn't, but raises another question: With such strong performance, why would you eliminate Utilities and Consumer Staples as possible buy candidates from the sector rotation universe?

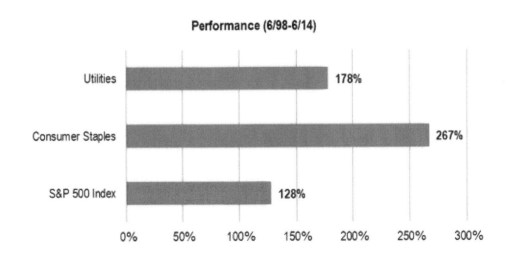

Performance (6/98-6/14)

Utilities — 178%

Consumer Staples — 267%

S&P 500 Index — 128%

0%   50%   100%   150%   200%   250%   300%

Authors' response: Your observation is good, on the surface it appears that the decision to exclude these 'defensive' sectors from the 'growth' universe does not make sense. However, we are operating under the assumption that times have changed; the stock market is in a new secular bull not a secular bear.

Jerry: How does that explain not including these two defensive sectors within the sector universe of possible buy candidates?

Authors' response: Utilities and Consumer Staples are considered great defensive sectors. Investors often favor these two during harsh economic times. The logic is when things are bad consumers still need electricity, water, heat, food, toilet paper, etc, and therefore investors move to sectors that are dependable. Also during market corrections investors will sell other sectors that depend upon discretionary spending like Leisure: consumers will delay that vacation and businesses will cut back on travel expenses.

During previous mega bull markets, corrections, even those associated with recessions, have been short and mild. The ongoing bull market quickly reasserts itself and equity markets move higher. Because that has been the historical pattern of cyclical bulls within a secular bull, we wanted the sector indexes to be quickly positioned into the leading growth sectors, not trapped and losing an investment opportunity by being invested in a 'defensive' sector.

During the inevitable market pullback, the defensive sectors will rise to the top of the relative strength rankings. Not because they are making large gains but simply by falling less than the rest of the market in most cases. We would be better off in money market fund. And then when the turnaround in the market occurs, the defensive sectors will at first be ranked the highest and become buy candidates. With only four sector buy candidates each quarter, the concern is the defensive sectors will block out the 'growth' sectors that will perform better in the new emerging cyclical bull market from the top four rankings.

Jerry: I see the logic; the defensive sectors only come into play at the end of short cyclical bear, maybe too late to help performance and could lower performance when the market turns up. Do you have any examples of this actually occurring or just a great theory?

	Utilities & Consumer Staples (Average)	Two Growth Sectors Pushed Out of Top Rankings (Average)
Q3 2011	-5.2%	-11.2%
Q4 2011	6.5%	0.9%
Q1 2012	2.2%	17.7%
Cumulative	3.2%	5.5%

Authors' response: We do, in the last bear market. From 4/11 through 9/11 the market fell just under 20% over five months, a short shallow bear market. By the end of June, the momentum/relative strength analysis was applied to find the leading sectors. If Utilities and Consumer Staples were included in the 'growth' sector universe they would have become buy candidates for the third and fourth quarters of 2011 and into the first quarter of 2012. They would have blocked out two 'growth' sectors as candidates. The table compares the returns of the Utility and Consumer Staples sectors versus the two growth sectors that they blocked out of the top four rankings.

Initially the defensive sectors (Utilities and Consumer Staples) added value over the growth sectors they replaced: in Q3 they fell but by less than half, and in Q4 they gained over 6% versus less than 1% for the growth sectors.

However, by Q1 2012, when the bull market was gaining momentum, the defensive sectors gained 3% but that was a mere shadow of the almost 18% gained by the missing growth sectors. Cumulative, the two growth sectors increased by almost 6% versus the 3% advance of the defensive sectors.

This is a pattern we would expect to be repeated during the coming secular bull: short small cyclical bears that would be quickly followed by bull markets. And during the bull markets, with an Aim Higher Goal of 1.5X the market, we did not want the sector indexes to be trapped in defensive sectors, instead they should be participating in the potential of the growth sectors.

Jerry: Thank you for the explanations, it does appear that the over performance is being added through the active rules (quarterly selection process, individual fund signals for risk management and using the Market Environment Indicator for adding leverage). I wish you continued success with the Sector Growth Index and Ultra Sector Index and would love to see and participate in another secular bull market.

Thank you and congratulations on Flexible Plan Investments being recognized by Financial Times as one of the 300 Top Registered Investment Advisors in the Nation. You, your staff and dynamic risk-managed investment solutions deserve it.

FOURTH MESSAGE

Plan your work, work your plan!

- Strength in diversifying over multiple active indexes.
- Perspective, Staying on Track and Winning
- What if we are wrong?
- Ongoing support: Monthly Newsletter, Website
- About the Authors
- Acknowledgments

"You were born to win, but to be a winner, you must plan to win, prepare to win, and expect to win."

—Zig Ziegler

"Create a definite plan for carrying out your desire and begin at once, whether you ready or not, to put this plan into action."

—Napoleon Hill

"No matter how carefully you plan your goals they will never be more than pipe dreams unless you pursue them with gusto."

—W. Clement Stone

Active Index Summary

The markets are in a new mega super boom! The Dow is headed to 85,000! The S&P 500 to 8880! Both are expected to show 700% gains over the coming two decades.

With history as our guide, we know that some indexes will outperform and others underperform. Looking back at the last secular bull, $100,000 invested in the S&P 500 would have grown to almost $1,500,000. Impressive. However, the same investment invested in the NASDAQ would be worth more than twice that or $3,100,000. Extremely impressive.

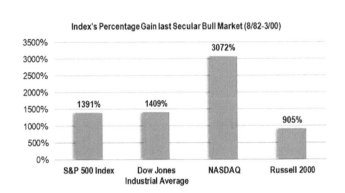

Index's Percentage Gain last Secular Bull Market (8/82-3/00)

Which one would you want to have owned? Naturally, all of us would immediately point to the NASDAQ! Who wouldn't want $3 million instead of $1.5 million?

There are two problems with that answer: First, none of us knew in 1982 exactly which index would be the next big winner, and second, would you have been able to stick with your chosen index for the duration?

The second problem is the hardest to solve. Say you had picked the NASDAQ, here are several hurdles you would have faced.

The NASDAQ on its 3000% run had four separate bear markets with an average loss of almost 33%. On four separate occasions you would have lost 1/3 of your investment. That is hard to stomach with losses greater than any of the other indexes. Next, after watching 1/3 of your capital disappear during the 1984-87 bull market, the NASDAQ underperformed the S&P significantly, another big emotional test of your decision to stick with the NASDAQ.

Solution, diversify among the stock indexes would still have generated S&P 500 Index beating performance...

But there's a better way!

Active Index Summary

We have introduced four active indexes, all striving for higher returns in rising markets and reducing risk in falling markets. Half of the indexes use no leverage to achieve their goal. Half can use leverage, seeking magnified returns. We believe any of the four can achieve the Aim Higher goal.

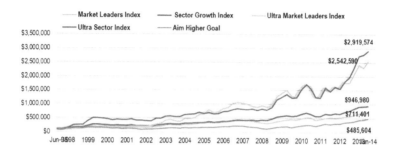

So, which index will be the absolute leader during the current super boom? We do believe that each of the four active rules based indexes will reach the Aim Higher Goal of +2100%. Logic favors the two Ultra indexes to outperform either of the two growth indexes.

But potential over performance alone shouldn't dictate a choice.

Being able to emotionally manage drawdown's and periods of relative under performance will impact one's ability to stick with a chosen index over time.

Therefore, blending of active indexes to meet investment goals and risk tolerance over a specific time horizon should be considered to manage the danger of poor emotion based decision making or just bad luck in your choice of a single index.

Risk and Return

A misplaced market myth is that high returns only come with higher risk. Not true. All four indexes have a historical record of higher returns with less risk. Within all four indexes risk management is a major part of the rules based index construction and it has paid off.

Beta is the measurement of a security's returns in response to swings in the market. A beta of 1 indicates that the security's price will move with the market. A beta of less than 1 means that the security will be less volatile than the market and greater than 1 will be more volatile than the market. For example, if a stock's beta is 1.2, it's theoretically 20% more volatile than the market. With the Aim Higher indexes all

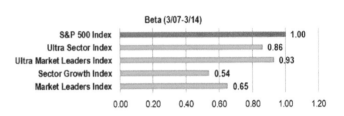

having annualized returns of 3-5X greater than the market you would expect a higher level of volatility-Beta. Not so; all four indexes had betas 10% to almost 50% less than the markets!

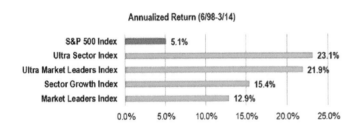

One other measurement of historical volatility is standard deviation (SD). For example, a volatile stock will have a high standard deviation while the deviation of a stable blue chip stock will be lower. A large dispersion tells us how much the return on the fund is deviating from the historical annualized return.

SD should be viewed in relationship to its annualized return. The market gained on average 5% and had a SD of 17%, or 3X its annualized return, a large variance.

In contrast both ultra indexes and Sector Growth had a SD almost equal to their annualized return, or 1X, one-third less variance than the S&P 500.

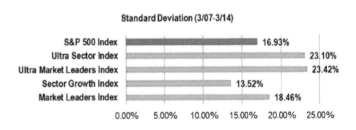

Historically, all four rules based Aim Higher indexes were able to provide higher returns with less risk!

50/50 Growth Indexes

One example is a simple 50% blend of both growth indexes: Market Leaders and Sector Growth.

Below are a couple of observations:

The investment experience was smoother. Overall the drawdown years for the 50/50 were more manageable than either index individually:

- The 2008 decline for 50/50 was half of the Market Leaders.
- The two year loss for Sector Growth in 2001 and 2002 was -12% versus less than -5% for the 50/50 combination.

Interestingly, at the end of 2007 the 50/50 combination was actually ahead in cumulative performance than either of the two growth indexes! The cumulative gain for the 50/50 combination was 6X the gain for the S&P 500 Index, and exceeded the Aim Higher goals by twice!

We are not making a recommendation on a 50/50 allocation. We only want to point out that combining indexes can lead to excellent performance with a smoother investment return. It is up to the advisor to determine the allocation mix that would best serve an individual client.

At either www.stirreserach.com or www.dow85000aimhigher.com all the monthly index return data is available. Advisors can mix and match different allocations of different indexes for their own study.

50/50 Ultra Indexes

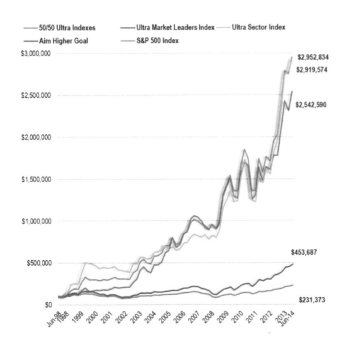

In 8 out of the 15 years illustrated the cumulative performance from the combination of the Ultra Indexes 50/50 outperformed either of the Ultra Indexes alone!

Another benefit? The drawdown years were smoother than the two individually:

- The 2008 decline for 50/50 was 60% less than the Ultra Market Leaders.
- The two year loss for Ultra Sector in 2001 and 2002 was -13% versus a gain of 2% for the 50/50 combination.

The cumulative gain for the 50/50 ultra indexes exceeded the Aim Higher goal by 7 times! The 50/50 ultra combination is well diversified: owning up to four asset classes and four sectors when bullish, each with its own Individual Fund Signal and employing the Market Environment Indicator to determine when to judiciously utilize ultra funds.

Again, we are not making a recommendation on a 50/50 allocation. We are only illustrating that combining indexes could possibly overcome bad luck or investor behavior of abandoning a good plan during a period of drawdowns or during a period of relative under performance.

Or, Combining a Growth Index with an Ultra Index

The choice does not have to be "do you want a maximum equity exposure of 100% or 200% (growth versus ultra)?"

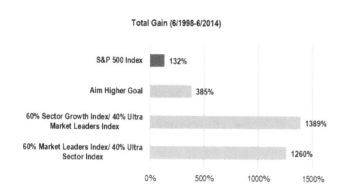

You can combine a growth index with an ultra index to give you a blend with just the right amount of maximum exposure desired.

Want an equity portfolio that wouldn't exceed 140% invested? Combine a 60% growth index and 40% of an ultra index. Mix and match the indexes based upon preferences of Market Leaders versus sectors.

Or, you like each index and simply want to own them all! A 25% allocation to each index would result in a portfolio that could have a Maximum Equity Exposure of 150%, hopefully during rising markets and striving to only have a 13% Equity Exposure during the worst of times. The chart below illustrates the potential of combining the 4 Aim Higher Indexes.

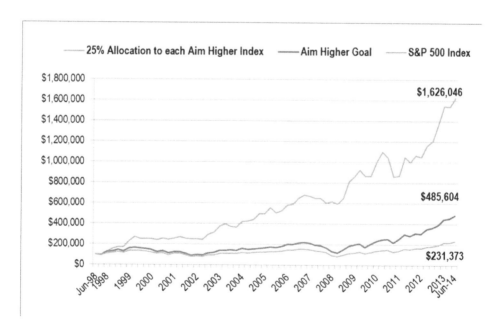

The combinations and variations are numerous. That is the beauty of four different indexes, combining the best qualities of each to meet the investment goals and risk tolerance for individual clients. No one size fits all.

Summary of Indexes

The market is in a new secular bull market. It is a new mega boom market that will carry the Dow and S&P 700% higher over the coming decades.

The Aim Higher Goal was to do better, **three times (3X) better:** a realistic goal if you can achieve just 50% better in the rising markets and do not lose more than the market in the down moves. Skeptics will say it is not possible, but we have introduced you to four different active rule based indexes that have done that and more (6/98-6/14):

- Market Leaders Index   8X
- Sector Growth Index   11X
- Ultra Market Leaders Index   33X
- Ultra Sector Index   38X

This research was accomplished over a historical time frame that included a 12 year secular bear with two declines of over -50%. Our forecast is for a secular bull, where the declines have historically been few and far between and when they do occur are in the low -20% to high teens, not in the -50% losses.

If the active Indexes can reach the Aim Higher Goals during such a difficult investment time in the past of little growth, couldn't we expect that they would again surpass the Aim Higher Goal of 3X in an upward pro-growth investment environment? We believe the answer to be yes!

"Discipline is the bridge between goals and accomplishment."

—Jim Rohn

So, if you were to follow a strategy built around any one of these indexes, which one should you choose? We directed these questions to Trent Schield, who has had almost two decades working with clients and advisors across the nation.

Q: How would you pick an index or strategy to follow?

Trent: That wouldn't be the question I would start with. I would ask 'what does it take to be a successful investor?'

First, investors need to be truly honest with themselves. Most do not have the time, the education, the experience and/or the mental discipline to succeed in the stock market. That is difficult to admit for many.

Second, the key then becomes finding the best possible investment advice. Investors need the broad financial services of a well trained, experienced advisor who embraces active management.

The third step then becomes matching strategies with the goals and risk tolerance of the investor.

Q: You said strategies not strategy, why not just one?

Trent: Building a great investment plan is like building a great football team. You need to have a solid offense scoring points, (in our case making money) and a solid defense not losing yardage (in our case not losing a lot of capital). That is your core. From that you add special teams or special plays to take advantage of certain circumstances. In the world of investing, you add 'explore' strategies to your core investment strategies.

Typically, the advisor ends up with a portfolio of one or two core equity strategies and adds several explore strategies. And the same is done on the bond side. But with a mega bull in stocks and probably a secular bear in bonds, the greatest upside potential is certainly on the stock side.

Q: But the indexes/strategies are diversified and have strong offenses and defenses already so still more than one?

Trent: Yes. Call it strategy diversification or as a great advisor in Texas called it "a happy portfolio." Every index or strategy will go through periods of over and under performance. If an investor has just one, it is emotionally harder to stick with a strategy or index, regardless of past success, when it is going through a rough period. However, if the investor has multiple active strategies in a single portfolio working for him/her, there is always the possibility that something else is working, and offsetting a period of underperformance elsewhere.

Q: Any other great ideas gathered out in the field from other successful advisors?

Trent: Yes, and too many to name here. We would have to write another book! But one of the key problems is addressing bad behavior in investors.

Another great advisor, also from Texas calls it his "5 legged stool" approach. Analogy; if you go to a bar and you see a 3, 4, and 5 legged stool and you are a 500 pound dude, which stool would you plop your behind on? You are going with the 5 legged stool.

Let's say you are a really scared investor. Think back to all the crises over the past decade: 9/11, Lehman Brothers bankruptcy, recessions, European sovereign debt crisis, government shutdowns, etc. Nothing is going well and you have 500 pound of worry on your back. You have a half million dollars to invest. Which stool are you're going to pick.....you will go back to the five.

You're combing actively managed strategies, I call it strategic diversification. The goal is to avoid emotional decision making by investors. No client ever fired anyone because of a strategy's beta, or lack of alpha. Most do not even know the definition of those words. They quit because of a strategy's lay down (lack of good relative performance) or draw down (losses). So, I'm going to build a 5 legged stool that minimizes those two things. I can't change investor behavior, but with strategic diversification I strive to reduce the possibility of the problems arising.

Thanks Trent, for sharing those thoughts.

Perspective

Keeping focused, keeping on track and sticking with active indexes will be difficult at times. Strong emotions will come into play at times. You will see better alternatives and be tempted to change course. Typically this will occur at the worst possible moment. When this does occur, we recommended reading the following thoughts before making any dramatic changes in your investment path.

The path to achieving investment success is to study long-term results (which hopefully this book has provided) and find a strategy (index) or group of strategies (indices) that make sense . Remember to consider risk and choose a level that is acceptable. Then stay on the path.

To succeed, let history guide you. Successful investors look at history. They understand and react to the present in terms of the past. Something as simple as looking at an index's best and worst periods during an advance or decline is a good example. Knowing the potential parameters of an index gives the investor a tremendous advantage over the uninformed. If the maximum expected loss is 35% and the indexes are down 15%, instead of panicking, an informed investor can feel happy that things aren't as bad as they could be. Being armed with this knowledge tempers expectations and emotions, giving informed investors a perspective that acts as an emotional pressure value.

Hopefully, all the data and guidance found in this book gives you perspective. It should help you understand that hills and valleys are part of every investment plan and are to be expected, not feared. Do not second guess. Do not change your mind. Do not try to outsmart. Looking over the past four or five bull and bear periods, you see that the indexes individually had periods in which they did not do as well as the market or met the AIM Higher expectations, but also had many periods in which they did much better. Understand that. Focus on the long term and let it work.

If you do, your chance of succeeding is very high. If you do not, no amount of knowledge will save you and you'll find yourself with the 80% of underperformers, thinking: What went wrong?

Paraphrased from "What Works on Wall Street" by James P. O'Shaughnessy

Perspective

Historically, <u>the average investor earns less than the market!!!</u> Almost 60% less. Over a 20 year period the S&P 500 Index averaged 9% a year, not a bad return. Unfortunately, the average equity investor earned a market return of less than 4%. Stated in dollars, a $100,000 investor account would have grown to $210,000 while the same investment in the market would be $570,000.

Why so poorly? Emotional investing by investors! *"The moment you start to second-guess your decisions is usually when you shouldn't."* **Troy Schield, Disciplined Wealth Management.**

Emotional Decisions: Investor versus Market/ Growth of $100,000
(12/90-12/10)

The active indexes have 4 basic principles in common that lead to long term success:

1. **Active**: they are not fixed; they are active, reacting to new trends.
2. **Risk Management**: they all have strong defenses; conservation of capital is a priority during the inevitable market declines.
3. **Discipline:** each index is driven by pre-determined time tested rules. Decisions are driven by rules, not emotions.
4. **Data Driven:** the indexes rely on hard numbers, actual trends, focusing on what the data is signaling, not driven by investor emotions.

Advisors and investors need to add two other essentials to be successful:
- **Patience:** let the long term work for you. A mega bull market is in progress; do not allow short term setbacks (which will occur) derail a proven disciplined plan.
- **Perspective:** keep your eyes on the long term goals. Stay on target and you will have a significantly better chance of achieving than those whose only plan is buy and hope.

Do not be guilty of benchmark shopping. There will be times when an index(s) will underperform a different index (benchmark). In fact, **at any time** an investor will be able to find some benchmark (bonds, real estate, gold, large cap stocks, small cap stocks, internationals, etc) that is performing better than the Market Leaders Index, or the Ultra Market Leaders Index, or the Ultra Sector Index or the Sector Growth Index.

Do not fall into that emotional decision making process. Stick with active indexes that have proven principles that lead to long term success.

Nervous about Leverage?

Leverage, in the case of ultra funds, where you are striving for 2X the daily percentage move of an index, can work for you or against you. We believe it is an appropriate tool to maximize gains and with a secular bull market acting as a strong tailwind, now is the opportune time to employ it.

But when wrong, it will generate larger losses than if not used. That is obviously the biggest concern. The table shows the historical average drawdown while the market was falling, the maximum drawdown (the largest single drawdown in 16 years) and the cumulative gain for the four active indexes.

	Risk		Reward	
	Average Drawdown last Four Bear Markets (Monthly Data)	Maximum Drawdown (Monthly Data)	Average Gain last Four Bull Markets	Cumulative Gain (6/98-6/14)
Market Leaders Index	-16%	-34%	100%	611%
Sector Growth Index	-13%	-18%	107%	847%
Ultra Market Leaders Index	-16%	-30%	197%	2440%
Ultra Sector Index	-19%	-32%	218%	2820%
S&P 500 Index	-33%	-53%	76%	131%

- As one would expect, under the maximum drawdown column, the Ultra indexes had larger losses than the unleveraged sector growth.
- Unexpected, the Market Leaders Index had a larger maximum drawdown than its ultra cousin. One explanation, the Ultra Market Leaders Index has two levels of risk management versus just one for Market Leaders.
- All the indexes employ risk management and therefore it is no surprise that both their average and maximum drawdowns were significantly less than the benchmark S&P 500 Index.

And before you say "I don't think I could use an ultra index," consider the overwhelming fact **that the average drawdown for the benchmark (-33%) was worse than the maximum drawdown for either of the ultra indexes.** The average investor in the S&P 500 Indexfor the past 16 years has suffered an average bear market loss greater than the one-time maximum drawdown of either of the ultra indexes!

Past performance is no guarantee of future performance, and that also applies to risk levels and possible drawdowns. From the data we can see that the extra set of risk management "brakes" we have put on the Ultra Indexes were able to keep the losses to less than the markets but not at the expense of growth on the upside.

What if we are wrong?

Good news. If we are wrong, you should still come out ahead.

Four ways we could be wrong:

1. Totally wrong, the secular bear market is not nearly over.
2. Too early, one last bear market to go before the start of a new mega bull market.
3. Mega bull is shorter and smaller than predicted.
4. Mega bull is longer and bigger.

Totally Wrong

What if the secular bear market that began in March 2000 is not even close to being finished? The 1929-49 U.S. secular bear lasted 20 years! Japan has been in a secular bear market since the end of 1989, which is 24 plus years and counting.

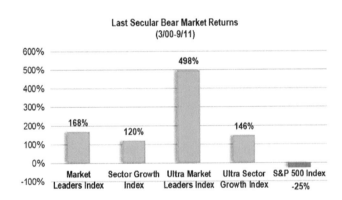

Instead of the secular bear being over in 11 years (2000-2011) in the outlook, what if it is only half way done? What if we have a repeat of the past secular pattern for another decade and the current rally (2011-14) is just another cyclical bull within an ongoing secular bear?

Answer, it would again be another terrible 11 years, with multiple bear market drops and bull rallies. Buy and Hope investors could again end up with no gains, only more frustration, and unfulfilled retirement dreams.

The chart illustrates the performance of Aim Higher Indexes (Market Leaders, Ultra Market Leaders, Sector Growth, and Ultra Sector) along with the S&P 500 from the high in 2000 to the low in 2011, from peak to trough.

If we are totally wrong and currently the market is at just another peak, with more bad news to follow, it will not be the story we truly expect to see unfold, but at the same time, it may not be the end of the world. While past performance is never a guarantee of future performance, the active indexes were able to navigate successfully the past secular bear over that 11 year period and produced triple digit gains.

What if we are wrong?

Too Early

This wouldn't be terrible news. In 1980 it appeared the market had broken out from a 12 year secular bear. The S&P made new highs, but a new recession derailed the bull market. A new bear market followed pushing prices down by 28% into the final low in 1982. Absent another recession, the probable worst case is the market may have one more mild bear market like in 2011. It was short, only five months, and mild, -20% versus the dual -50% declines of the previous decade.

- Keep in mind that each of the four active indexes has strong defenses. They strive to reduce the negative impact of market declines by making defensive moves to the safety of bonds or money markets.
- Also, if we are one down market away from the start of the next mega bull market, it gives you more time to prepare, to get in position.

What if we are wrong?

Mega bull is shorter and smaller.

That would be disappointing but possible. We believe all the evidence is present that a new mega secular bull market has begun. The past two secular bulls each lasted almost two decades, with one gaining 700%, the other 1400%. Historically the market rallies 2/3rds of the time and only falls 1/3rd. Given the last two secular bear markets lasted 14 and 12 years, or 1/3rd of the time, the new mega bull life should be around 18 to 20 years. That is why we made our estimate for a move into 2030.

You have to go back almost 100 years to find a secular bull market shorter than the one we envision: the Dow (S&P 500 yet to be invented) from a low in 1921, rose + 500% over eight years. So if it is shorter and therefore smaller in total gain, if it lasts only 8 years and only gains 500%, that makes employing active indexes even more important. If you can not rely on just buying and holding and getting 500% to reach your goals, you need to step up your investments, Aim Higher and make the absolute most of the opportunity is given.

Mega bulls last longer with bigger gains!

This would be the best way to be wrong. We would love to see a repeat of the 1982-2000 mega secular bull that gained 1400%. It would only take one more good cyclical bull market move to take our projection of a +700% gains and turn it into a +1400% move. This would give extra years for the active indexes to add even more value. Following that logic, the active indexes total return could also double!

That the Dow will close exactly at 85,000 on December 31, 2030 is probably extremely doubtful. No one can be that precise in looking forward for the next two decades. The bigger point is that we are in a new secular bull market that will probably last for many years and have spectacular gains. You do not want to miss out on or settle for just market returns, Aim Higher!

Dow85000AimHigher.com

Want to keep updated on the new mega secular bull as it fights it way to 85,000 by 2030?

The big upward move will not be accomplished in one long steady climb. That would be too easy, and making money never comes that easy. This mega bull will be interrupted by the occasional bear market decline and recession that will shake your confidence.

Imagine getting on that plane for the vacation with spouse and family long dreamed of. At first you're excited that your journey has begun, and also a little nervous. As the plane speeds down the runway, wheels lift off, and you start to rise. As you climb higher to your cruising altitude you will probably hit a couple of air pockets, some so violent to make you grab the arm rest or your companion. You may even have second thoughts, "maybe we should have driven!" But this all passes. The pilot soon takes off the fasten seat belt sign, and the celebrated beverage cart comes around.

The pilot will come on and offer words of reassurance and guidance. He/she will explain what has occurred and what to expect.

www.Dow85000aimhigher.com

This is your pilot for the coming years. We want to offer that same level of service. We appreciate that you have purchased the book and we want to extend that education and guide you through the ups and downs of this mega secular bull market, so you won't miss out on what is happening.

We have created www.dow85000aimhigher.com, just click on for:
- Detailed explanations of the four active indexes: Market Leaders, Ultra Sector and Ultra Market Leaders and Sector Growth.
- A complimentary monthly letter
- Up dated performance and more.

Indexes: We provide detailed up to date explanations of the active indexes highlighted in this book. This can include updates and enhancements to the indexes.

Monthly letter (complimentary): Published shortly after month end. This covers activity for the past month, explanations on any index changes, and an outlook on what you might expect for the coming month.

- Simply sign on at the home page for the complimentary newsletter. You have our assurances that we do not sell, share or provide your email address to any third party.

Have Questions? As a subscriber (complimentary), you can submit questions. We do not provide personal advice. However, we appreciate questions or concerns, as it gives us general ideas or topics that we can address in the monthly letter.

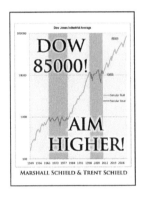

Need help? If an advisor was nice enough to give or suggested this book, seek out his/her advice for what is appropriate for you based upon your investment horizon and risk profile. They are the experts in financial planning.

The Authors, First Generation

Marshall Schield made his first investment at the age of 14 with the grand purchase of four shares of Cinerama at $4 a share. The stock was purchased in his own name (before the Uniform Gifts to Minors Act) and with help from his mother driving him to the brokers office. Months later, he cashed out doubling his money, and he was hooked on investing. Fortunately for Marshall he grew up with parents who were intelligent investors and encouraged him to pursue something he enjoyed.

After graduating from college in three years, he became the youngest stockbroker in the nation by age 21 in 1968. That year also marked the end of a secular bull (a general period of rising prices) in stocks and bonds and the start of a 14 year secular bear (falling prices). It was a quick and painful lesson during the first bear market fall of -36% from 1968-70 learning the importance of active investing (conserving wealth) versus buy and hope investing (loosing wealth).

As an active strategist for four decades, Marshall has achieved the following milestones:

- 1982 named one of the top four market timers for the prior decade by Money Magazine.
- Avoided the Crash of 1987 (prices fell over -25% in a single day), winning him recognition in Barron's Magazine, USA Today, and other national publications.
- In 1990, along with Troy Schield, managed the #1 Capital Appreciation fund according to Lipper Analytical Services.
- In 1997, authored the first book on sector fund investing, *Sector Funds for Trophy Returns*.
- One of only a handful of strategists that called the coming secular bear market of 2000-11, and acted on that knowledge with active strategies.
- Avoided the majority of both the 2000-02 and 2007-08 market declines.
- Participated in the majority of every major bull market since 1970.

Mr. Schield is the Chief Strategist for STIR Research LLC, a publisher of active allocation indexes and asset class/sector research for financial advisors and institutional investors. His major contribution to this book is in long term market trends (he has experienced the best and worst of markets) and research/development of active indexes.

The Authors, Second Generation

Trent Schield's indoctrination into active strategies began in his early teens. Taking a bus from school to his dad's office and then waiting for a ride home, his father, rather than watch his son disturb the hard working employees (he has a gift for engaging others in conversation) put him to work doing statistical research.

Later, it was time to build an internet site for advisors. At one of the company's annual conferences Trent was asked to introduce the internet site to +80 advisors. He was a natural, a born speaker. In understanding the basics of active strategies by listening in on conversations with advisors, he quickly learned how to convey the attributes of active strategies to advisors and to simplify the complex into easy to understand concepts for clients.

Based upon that talent, the logical next step after college was to become an internal wholesaler. But that was short lived, as the real experience was out in the field, not in the office. Also making more money for a growing family (three smart, fun, good looking and very active children: Cole, Vann, and Levi) with extensive hobbies (national BMX racing, wake boarding, travel, skiing, wrestling and foot-ball) was a great influence.

Trent has helped thousands of advisors understand the concepts and principles of active strategies, and more importantly, how to address the emotional decision making by clients that too often destroys well thought out investment programs. Trent has the experience of working one on one with

clients and addressing groups well into the thousands at national conventions.

With +20 years of experience, his greatest contributions to this book were in "Aim Higher" ("advisors and clients need to know that they can do better, much better, than simply buy and hold"), and his experience in combining active indexes, " what is needed is the right mixture of active strategies that smooth the ride and balance performance".

Lastly, his first "investment love," active sector allocation, was his encouragement to build upon two decades of sector investing experience: "the time is right, it's a perfect investment environment for active sector allocation to add significant over performance".

Trent Schield is Regional Sales Manager for the western region with Flexible Plan Investments, Ltd.

Acknowledgments

Sandra Schield, President of STIR Research LLC, for continuous moral support and editorial advice. Her lifetime experience from working with thousands of clients and hundreds of advisors helped in knowing how to convey the story clearly and in the presentation of the material.

Troy Schield, President of Disciplined Wealth Management, for his expert assistance and seasoned advice with the quantitative active indexes.

Milo Schield, (Marshall's brother), author of *Statistical Literacy* for constant encouragement and reviewing the arguments supported by the statistics for any errors in "confounding," or "is it mere association and not causation."

Steven Gray, for his expert assistance and for many hard hours spent on chart construction and most of all for his creativity, wisdom, and wit to push us through the final hours.

Renee Toth, Vice President of Flexible Plan Investments Ltd., for countless time spent editing.

Terra Toner, (Marshall's granddaughter) we thank for the talented and humorous art work.

Below is a short list of people that have influenced our quantitative philosophy over the years and/or moral support during trying times.

- Howard Hebert, Hebert Advisory Services
- Ned Davis, Tim Hayes and the entire NDR Group
- Dan Sullivan, The Chartist
- Jerry C. Wagner, Flexible Plan Investments
- Skip Viragh, Rydex founder
- Jeff Omdahl, a talented resource
- Corey Colehour, former NFL quarterback and great partner

CPSIA information can be obtained at www.ICGtesting.com
Printed in the USA
BVOW11s0059170914

367117BV00002B/2/P